Tradition of Craftsmanship
in MEXICAN HOMES

Seen through the high arch, two large antique wooden horses lead the visitor
to the vaulted entrance hall in the Pössenbachers' unique Cuernavaca Home.

TRADITION

of CRAFTSMANSHIP in

MEXICAN HOMES

Patricia W. O'Gorman

Photographs by Bob Schalkwijk

Architectural Book Publishing Company
TAYLOR TRADE PUBLISHING
Lanham • New York • Boulder • Toronto • Plymouth, UK

To Nina Lincoln and Peter Bubela
with our love

Architectural Book Publishing Company

Published by Taylor Trade Publishing
An imprint of The Rowman & Littlefield Publishing Group, Inc.
4501 Forbes Boulevard, Suite 200, Lanham, Maryland 20706
www.rowman.com

10 Thornbury Road, Plymouth PL6 7PP, United Kingdom

Distributed by National Book Network

Designed by Al Lichtenberg

The cloth edition of this book was previously catalogued by the Library of Congress. Catalog Card Number: 80-10254

ISBN 978-1-58979-800-7 (pbk. : alk. paper)
ISBN 978-1-58979-801-4 (electronic)

♾™ The paper used in this publication meets the minimum requirements of American National Standard for Information Sciences—Permanence of Paper for Printed Library Materials, ANSI/NISO Z39.48-1992.

Printed in the United States of America

Contents

Juan O'Gorman in his studio in Mexico City.

Foreword

It now seems clear that the International Style of modern architecture applied to residential buildings has worn out. Many families with an income high enough to own a house to live in do not want the sterile look of the elegant waiting room of a dentist's office for their homes. Most people are fed up with the mechanical so-called style of the Bauhaus commercial furniture. They are looking for ideas to make their houses gracious and comfortable places in which to live.

This book is a summary or compilation of houses, architectural details and furniture which give us the feeling of a friendly and pleasant atmosphere. You will find here a number of examples taken from Mexican Colonial Architecture that show the ambience of the houses of the old Spanish aristocracy, which were built during a time when every form of construction and all the appliances of a home were made by artists and artisans with the knowledge of their handicrafts and a love of beautiful objects.

In this book one can also find excellent examples of the Mexican popular art of building, much of it done with primitive methods that achieve great human dignity in their proportions and that provide ideas of form and color for interior decoration and furniture. Thanks to the natural talent of carpenters, masons and builders and houses in general, their simple constructions have remained faithful to their regional traditions. All the folk architecture that has been inherited from the past is an excellent source of inspiration to be applied and used to great advantage in modern houses because it has the necessary elements that are in accordance with the function and the climate of the region in which they were done. The regional methods of construction also achieve the beauty of natural simplicity which is not only more pleasant to live with, but also cheaper to make.

Therefore, this is a useful book which I hope will be of help and inspiration to the house owner as well as to the architect, the furniture maker, the craftsman and the artisan, in order to make houses, their furnishings and gardens more comfortable, and also provide a better surrounding and environment for daily human interest and enjoyment.

JUAN O'GORMAN

Acknowledgments

We wish to thank very specially Arquitecto Juan O'Gorman for his sustained interest and many helpful suggestions; Mr. Javier Tinoco for his indefatigable efforts in the photographic laboratory; and Mr. Peter Glenville for the time he so kindly spent helping the author.

Also, Mr. John Beadle, Mr. Jaume Ribas, Arquitecto René Escobosa, Mr. Levant Alcorn and Mr. Hardy William Smith, without whose help, talent and encouragement this book would never have been produced.

In addition, our warmest thanks to the many kind people who allowed us to photograph their homes and made it such a delightful experience.

Picture Locations

Tradition of Craftsmanship
in MEXICAN HOMES

ADOBE

THE USE OF ADOBE as a building material is common in the many arid and semi-arid regions of both Mexico and the United States since before Spanish Colonial times. It has been extensively used in the construction of both civil and religious buildings, such as the missions in the southwest of the United States, which still stand and bear witness to the enduring quality of this material in an appropriate setting and climate.

Due to the small number of Spanish settlers and natives living in these regions, and to the great amount of time and effort spent in maintaining a life constantly threatened by hardship and danger, adobe was chosen over the more time-consuming stone or brick and mortar construction.

The manufacture of adobe has remained the same in Mexico since it made its first appearance. Wet clay is kneaded with bare feet until it becomes a uniform paste. Then, cut straw or manure are added in order to keep it from cracking. It is then put into molds to dry in the sun for two or three days before it is ready to be used. Dry adobes are joined together with wet clay paste and held in place with small pebbles or fragments of brick.

The great enemy of adobe is moisture. Therefore, it is extremely rare in Mexico to find any original construction where the adobe shows on the outside. As soon as the walls, pillars, etc., are constructed, they are either plastered over or at least whitewashed to protect them from the rain. Nowadays, chemical preparations are available to seal adobe effectively, so that its true beauty and warm color is made apparent.

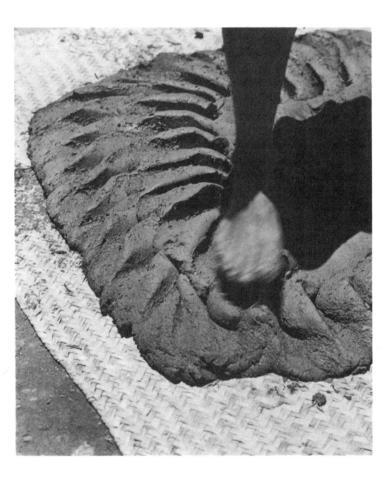

Opposite: This stately covered arcade in Alamos shows the possibilities of using adobe to great advantage when constructing intricate columns and arches that support a beamed ceiling.

Four different examples in which adobe can be seen by itself or in combination with brick, tile or stucco.

Above: This unusual two-story house recently built by Arquitecto Alejandro von Wuthenau against the dramatic backdrop of the impressive Tepoztlán crags blends in perfectly with the surrounding scenery.

Below: Over the brick cornice of the window, small fragments of stone set into mortar hold these adobes in place and make a pleasing pattern.

Home of Peter and Elisabeth Gerhard

Home of Peggy Regler

Bare adobe has recently become fashionable in combination with brick roof tiles and a graceful lattice screen as used here in these houses in Tepoztlán.

Home of Peter and Elisabeth Gerhard

3

Home of Peter and Elisabeth Gerhard

Already showing the sad effects of time and lack of protection, these old walls still stand on a street corner in San Miguel de Allende, where adobe continues to be used to build houses by its less affluent inhabitants and some of its eccentric foreign residents.

Below: Under cover of a beamed ceiling and completely protected from moisture, adobe lasts forever and gives its earthy warmth to this outdoor living area.

4

Oddly enough, adobe has also been used extensively in the town of Valle de Bravo, where the rains are very heavy.

Right: The stair guard of this house at the corner of Calle Culebra (Street of the Snake) is also made of adobe, the stair treads are lined with thinly cut hard stone and the pillar supporting the roof (an unfortunate new addition) is made of red brick.

A classic example of a native house built entirely of adobe in the town of Tonantzintla, near Puebla, is truly a delight because of its simplicity and the extraordinary use of color. The thick, square pillars are painted a delicate yellow with the capitals and cornices contrasting in a strong ochre. The interior of the corridor is washed in fascinating periwinkle blue and the dust guard (*guardapolvo*) is also painted the same ochre.

Rancho "La Soledad"

6 Inspired by the adobe architecture of Santa Fe, New Mexico,
this small eating recess in the guest house of Father Wall's
"Rancho La Soledad" gives a feeling of understated tranquility.

Two entrances set into adobe walls in Cuernavaca, the upper one is topped by a light reinforced concrete cornice which gives it added strength and ends attractively against the stuccoed doorframe in the shape of a large S.

Below: More elaborate is the elegant entrance to the house of the late owner of "Las Mañanitas." Here the antique wooden door is surrounded by a carved stone frame. A simple iron railing sets off the carved stone steps. The natural earth coloring of the adobe wall makes an appropriate background to this most beautiful garden.

"Las Mañanitas"

7

If one wishes to find utter perfection in adobe construction, the delightful town of Alamos in the State of Sonora in northwestern Mexico should be one's Mecca.

Alas, here it is all so beautifully protected, painted and well kept that one needs an act of faith to believe that all the pastel-shaded houses with their long cool *portales* and flowering oleanders are indeed made of this humble material. However, on entering any of these houses on a sweltering day, the advantages of building with adobe are soon apparent, since the interiors are always invitingly cool.

Complementing the massive adobe walls are the ingenious native *vara* (twig) ceilings which shade the inevitable and most welcome *portales* through which one walks everywhere in this dreamlike town.

"Casa del Obispo"

Under this gracefully arched, two-storied *portal*, one has a view of the delicate stone-work around the entrance door and windows of an adobe house known as the Casa del Obispo in Alamos. The light and shadow make constantly changing patterns on the old brownish-red tiled floor. The delicate iron grilles, looking like enormous bird cages, cover the upper windows and keep children from falling out and *señoritas* from eloping.

Home of Edward and Catherine Barnes

Sharing the same wide street, these four one-story adobe houses in Alamos are distinguished by the delicate stucco details on their façades. The street is lined on both sides by similar houses painted in artfully combined pastel tones to which much light is added by whitewashing the cornices and frames around the doors and windows. The effect of enchantment is completed by the flowering oleanders and feathery trees planted in front of every house.

Home of Herrick and Elisabeth Nuzom

In the outdoor corridors surrounding the charming patio of an old house, much entertaining is done year around under the *vara* ceilings supported by simple whitewashed stucco columns.

Often seen in Mexico is this method of joining four beams over a wooden support or stone column. The beams here are cut in the traditional *pecho de paloma* (pigeon breast) style. However, in more elaborate buildings the beams are sometimes lavishly carved in a great variety of designs.

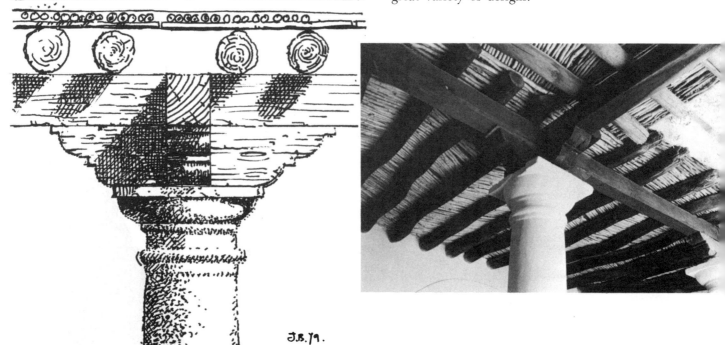

John Beadle 79.

The old, carved pink cantera fireplace in
the back *portal* of the Nuzoms' home was
brought to Alamos by the late Georgio Bel-
loli, the talented creator of many well-known
houses in Marfil, near Guanajuato. In spite of
its long voyage, it looks very much at home
here.

Home of Herrick and Elisabeth Nuzom

13

Alamos undoubtedly is a town of *portales*. These sensible covered areas, more than anything else, give it its unique flavor. In truly Spanish Colonial tradition, all communication between the rooms of the house is through these covered areas in order to respect privacy and because they provide welcome refuge from the sun and the rain. There is, therefore, scarcely a house in Alamos that does not possess both a *portal* on the street and one or several inside.

The house above, in its way, is the embodiment of the spirit of this region. The owners have really understood the essence of the adobe house, to which they have only added their own very personal distinction.

The shallow reflecting pool makes a refreshing focal point in the center of the grass courtyard at the back of which six white stucco columns on a mellow brick floor make an enchanting place in which to sunbathe.

Below: Several architectural elements make this small house an example of the typical Alamos home. It is built of adobe, the ceiling of the *portal* is made of *vara* and it is supported by whitewashed stucco pillars.

The iron railing over the window also follows the traditional style of Alamos by ending in little arrow points at the top.

14

Home of Mr. and Mrs. Cotton

In this XVIII century adobe house which has recently been reconstructed by its owners, wood has been used most imaginatively. Here, massive square beams and carved wooden corbels take the place of the usual stucco columns used to support the roofs.

15

Home of Mr. and Mrs. Cotton

JOHN BEADLE 79.

Opposite page: The unusual outdoor stairs that go up to the *mirador* (look out) are constructed of several thick wooden steps which are inserted from above at different angles over a central supporting pole.

One of the few remaining adobe houses still standing in Mexico City, la "Casa de los Camilos," in the beautiful district of Coyoacán, was once a *convento*. In this part of Mexico City, Hernán Cortez, the conqueror of Mexico, had his palace. Legend says that he had the huge ash trees planted on the main square and along all the important streets. This stately former *convento* has now been turned into a restaurant and a ceramic factory.

Below: The ravages of time are sadly apparent in this delightful adobe arcade in the village of Atotonilco, whose crowning glory is the XVIII century *Santuario* from which Don Miguel Hidalgo, the father of Mexican Independence, took up his banner with the image of the Virgin of Guadalupe.

18

"Hotel Alamos"

The architects in Spanish Colonial times took skillful advantage of the thickness of the walls. In those days, a single adobe measured up to 11″ by 19″ by 5″ and weighed up to 66 pounds. This allowed for many interesting construction features, such as recessed windows and doors and the famous *nichos de concha* (shell niches). This double arch in the colonial two-story Hotel Alamos served to form a seat and the entrance to the stairs.

19

STONE

THE WORD STONE immediately conjures up a hard and unsympathetic image. However, in the hands of the skilled craftsmen of Mexico, it emerges as the most majestic and enduring of all building materials. In Spanish Colonial times, stone was used not only for building walls but also for many of the ornamental details of the great houses of the day.

In Mexico, several types of stone are quarried for the purpose of carving decorative features. The Spanish word for this type of stone is *cantera*, and it exists in different colors and textures. The hard grey is considered the best, followed by the brown, pink, green, yellow and apricot. The craftsmen who work this stone are called *canteros* and these magicians perform miracles with their hammers and chisels. Birds, flowers, animals and even humans are given life by their skill and talent.

Maestro Antonio Vazquez, of a well-known family of *canteros* in San Miguel de Allende, shows in his work the tradition of excellence he has inherited from his Indian and Spanish ancestors.

The former *convento* of San Martín de Huaquechula in the State of Puebla shows two different ways in which stone can be used in the same building. The walls are built of massive blocks of stone into which this square niche is recessed. The imposing sobriety of this XVI century building is relieved by the delicately carved plaque depicting a rather large Saint Martin cutting his cloak and giving half of it to the very thin pauper while the horse looks on with obvious approval.

21

The very best that Mexico has to offer has been transported to San Antonio, Texas and transformed into the breathtaking house of Mr. and Mrs. Marshall Steves, Sr. Their archi-tect shows not only his impeccable taste but also his great understanding of things Mexi-can. In these warm and amiable surroundings, the many beautiful objects in Mrs. Steves' extensive collection look happy and at home.

Below: These specially made open-work *can-tera* carvings are ingeniously used as discreet vents for the air conditioning system; a great improvement on those made commercially.

The grand old XVIII century wooden doors, set into an impressive carved brownish-pink stone frame, give access to the main hall.

In the center of a most impressive high-ceilinged *sala*, the delicately carved XVIII century fireplace gives great warmth to the room in every sense of the word. The fireplace is elegantly complemented by the French brass andirons and the well-displayed glowing and colorful tin *santos*.

Home of Marshall and Patsy Steves

Two angels, musicians, stand on the hearth and make this fireplace in the master bedroom of the Steves' San Antonio home a thing of joy and gaiety.

23

Home of Marshall and Patsy Steves

24

Looking through these soaring XVII century arches brought from colonial Morelia, one gets a breathtaking vista of the large main patio. Authentic Mexican flowerpots filled with blooming red geraniums are ranged around the inevitable stone fountain.

These two beautiful animal representations are part of the world-famous archeological collection of Mr. and Mrs. Josué Saenz.

The connoisseur in his travels discovers four interesting examples of stone carvings from the early transition period shortly after the Spanish conquest. Native carvers at this time still gave their work a markedly indigenous stamp, although they tried to conform to Spanish designs.

A pre-Columbian serpent's head is used here as the cornerstone of an early colonial town house in Mexico City.

Beautifully carved, this stone fragment, which might have come from an important temple or palace, depicts the head of a *Caballero Aguila* (an Aztec warrior) and is now used as an ornament in a simple village house in Cholula, near Puebla.

Left: This high relief on an old stone wall is probably one of the earliest representations of the Mexican national emblem: the eagle standing on a *nopal* (cactus) devouring a serpent. The legend below is partly written in native characters and partly in Spanish.

An unusual form of design called *tequitqui* finds its most eloquent expression here. This relief sculpture on the facade of a house in Puebla is an amusing combination of anachronistic styles and was almost certainly inspired by a Gothic tapestry.

Extremely exciting for the stroller in Mexico are the many treasures he discovers as he walks through the streets of the many fascinating Colonial towns and cities. Finding unassuming stone carvings such as these gives him a personal sense of discovery.

Above: In many old towns in Mexico the hallowed tradition was to place little stone niches with either a cross or a saint in the street corner of the house.

Left: This simple plateresque stone madonna is set into a street wall in the romantic San Angel district of Mexico City. Added to the blessings that it brings to the house, placing religious images on the street has the added advantage that people do not throw the garbage nearby, but contain their impatience and await the truck for *basura.*

Over a doorway in Querétaro Saints Peter and Paul smilingly guard the entrance to the house surrounded by a beautifully carved, feathery garland.

Not far away, one comes upon this slightly damaged but still proud redstone lion set into the terracotta wall behind the market fountain in Quéretaro. From here he watches the fruit and vegetables being washed in the stone basin below and sold across the street.

Below: Primitive and very old, this unusual mermaid surfaces as the cornerstone of a building in San Cristóbal de las Casas.

The small stone sailing ship carved in delicate relief in the city of Campeche is probably a reminder of the fascinating seafaring tradition of this city.

With few exceptions the façades of the houses in the city
of Querétaro boast of one or
more balconies facing the street.
These imaginative carved stone
corbels in the shape of strange
beasts adorn the more elaborate
buildings and remind one of
medieval gargoyles.

Querétaro is a wonderful city
to visit if one wishes to en-
counter authentic architectural
treasures of the Spanish Colonial
period. As one walks through its
many stone-paved streets, one
finds houses such as the *"Casa
de la Columna"* (House of the
Column) where, as its name indicates, a simple tall column
supports the center of the corner balcony.

In order to give prominence to the entrance, builders in Mexico traditionally place a stone carving or any other eye-catching feature over the main doorway. A tall ornately carved stone *copete* gives this door in Alamos a feeling of importance.

Home of Dr. Mario González Ulloa

Above: Dr. Mario González Ulloa, with his usual flair, designed this charming pair of flowery angels over the entrance door of his home in San Miguel de Allende.

Inspired by an XVIII century French brass ornament and beautifully translated into stone, this flower basket over yet another doorway extends a warm welcome.

Home of Alfred and Nika Fleissig

Delicately carved out of stone of various colors and textures, these three openings give light to usually dark churches, making full decorative use of the width of the massive stone walls.

Ojos de buey, from the French *Oeil de Bœuf,* can be round or oval and they are still ingeniously used in colonial type buildings (*above and lower left*).

Below: Claraboyas (quatrefoil windows) also adorn many Colonial edifices and give added light when placed at a great height. These, too, have been adopted by some of today's builders, who think that just one of these windows, however haphazardly placed, makes the house look "Colonial."

Home of Ignacio and Guadalupe Iturbe

In contrast to the floridity of the bull's eyes, and *claraboyas*, the simplicity of this window frame and its counterparts in an elegant street in San Miguel de Allende is very refreshing.

35

Massive simplicity is the keynote of early Colonial architecture. In most buildings of this period the walls are of an incredible width, sometimes measuring up to six feet. This width made it possible for the builders of those times to recess the doors, windows, niches and stairs in a most imaginative manner.

Holding on for dear life, this stone lion spouts water into the basin of a large and impressive fountain in the center of Puebla's main square.

On a street corner between two charming houses, this primitive grey stone angel looks effective against the light yellow of the wall. Angels are a favorite subject of Mexican popular artists because they consider them to be bearers of good tidings.

Home of David and Anne Wilson

Seemingly carrying the heavy cornice on his head, this whimsical caryatid does much to lighten the severe facade of a building in Guanajuato.

37

Proclaiming Cuernavaca a city of gardens, the carved stone door frame with its floral motif is aptly surrounded by the ever-present *moneda* vine.

This arched doorway in Mexico City forms part of the stone garden wall in the background. Only the cornices protrude slightly from the square-cut pillars on both sides. The delicately carved keystone adds a graceful touch.

Stone is used throughout in the construction of this new house in San Miguel de Allende. The street façade and the frame around the door show that the same kind of stone can be worked in several ways. The wall is constructed with rough pieces of brown soft stone combined with hard stone, fragments of brick and any similar odds and ends to reproduce the appearance of early Colonial walls. In contrast, the finely carved frame and the niche over the door, made of the same soft brown stone, show the fine hand of the carver.

Ground Floor Scale 1:100

The most important decorative feature in the entrance hall is this large open-work stone carving showing Adam and Eve under the apple tree. Inspired by an old German woodcut, the Mexican craftsman's interpretation is most amusing.

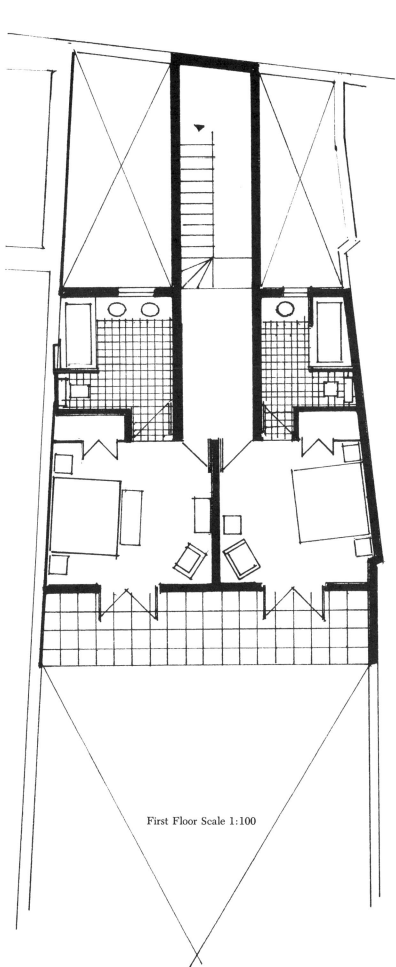

First Floor Scale 1:100

The garden façade is daily set aglow by the afternoon sun which warms and mellows the stone walls. Brick has been used here to frame the doors and windows and to form the cornices. Its reddish-brown natural color relieves the austerity of the stone.

41

Two allegorical female stone figures form the background to this enchanting fountain in the garden of the Yonkers'. Probably salvaged from the demolition of a turn-of-the-century building by Xavier Barbosa, who designed and built the house and who knows how to place these carved stone ornaments to unexpected advantage.

Angels in an unimaginable variety of styles appear in churches, public squares and private gardens in Mexico. This archangel Saint Raphael, in the garden of Mr. and Mrs. Rosenzweig Díaz, is a specially fine specimen of the celestial host. From its pierced iron halo, water cascades into the small basin at its feet.

Home of Susie Noel

Nature is always a great source of inspiration to the stone carver in Mexico. Flowers, fruit and all sorts of real and imaginary animals come to life through his skill. The urn standing over a balustrade and the plaque set into the rough stone wall are both the work of the same craftsman, Maestro Juan Vazquez of San Miguel de Allende.

Translated into stone in native style, these cherubs of Italian ancestry make an amusing subject for the open-work carving that gives light and ventilation to a garden potting shed.

Totally primitive, the holy water font in the church of Atotonilco is carved out of hard grey stone. The detail above it is molded out of stucco.

Home of David and Anne Wilson

From the majestic growling lion to the motherly clucking hen, no animal is too humble to be given loving tribute by the Mexican craftsman. The lion is a traditional ornament in Spanish Colonial buildings and gardens. As king of beasts he was much loved by the proud Spanish conquerers. Stone rabbits and chickens are not easily found. This charming rabbit was copied from a French XVIII century engraving and the hen was bought by its owner at a native Mexican market.

Home of Peter and Patricia Bubela

Home of Edward and Juliet Yonkers   *Home of Susie Noel*

Mexico enjoys such unsurpassed good weather that almost all houses possess one or more outdoor living areas, where it is possible to escape the hot sun while enjoying the feeling of being outdoors. Different types and colors of stone have been used to build the wall partially surrounding this outdoor *sala*. The antique columns and stone dolphins on the hood of the fireplace are also carved in stone.

Peering through luscious climbing geraniums, a white stone lamb looks enchanting in the center of the small brick-paved terrace.

Home of Antonio and Francesca Saldivar

To find an XVIII century partly ruined stone house in the middle of Mexico City is to be fortunate indeed; but to have talented Arquitecto Alejandro von Wuthenau to restore it is divine luck. Such is the combination that makes Mr. and Mrs. Antonio Saldivar's home so unique. The entrance has been kept as authentic as possible and any additions are totally in character with the original building. The tall wooden doors are also of the same period.

Home of Michael and Nicolette Pössenbacher

Not only as an ornament but as a constructive element, stone imparts great elegance and beauty to architecture both past and contemporary. Here, in striking contrast to the massive masonry walls, is the delicacy of the paving of the driveway in a Cuernavaca home. *Piedra bola* (round paving stones) are placed in geometric patterns around squares of hard white *cantera*.

The boundary wall and the stone pilasters, each made in a different pattern, say much for Mr. Pössenbacher's daring and impeccable taste.

48

Two round stone carvings are set into the walls of the XVI century Franciscan former *convento* of Coatlinchán. They were obviously found nearby and used as building stones. One represents the sun, a vital religious symbol for the natives; the other has the initials of Christ carved on it.

Without the aid of mortar or any other binding substance to hold these stones together, the natives of Alamos have built a long dry stone wall to surround Mrs. Heywood's extensive property. Their skill probably is inherited from Indian ancestors who built, in the same way, the ancient marvels we admire today.

Home of Martha Heywood

Lying prostrate on the ground like a gigantic jig-saw puzzle, this façade of a demolished building waits for an inspired architect to put it up again and restore it to its former glory. Dr. Mario González Ulloa, with great artistry and vision, has created a home for these derelicts that would otherwise succumb ignobly to the XX century's bulldozing civilization.

In order to integrate this "S" shaped buttress with the façade, it was buillt with the same stone as the wall and then carved by a stonemason with fluting which gives it a feeling of depth.

Ex-Hacienda Museo de San Gabriel de Barrera

An unusual find in the gardens of the former hacienda Museo de San Gabriel de Barrera near Guanajuato is this high window made of polished thin stone slabs. Set in sideways and used as bars, they form a *celosía* window much favored in Colonial country houses.

Hacienda de Ojo Caliente

The stonemason has taken great pains to make his work attractive by filling the joints between the stones with chips of the same color.

51

Home of David and Anne Wilson

Highly decorative is this old, light-colored stone frame around the French door leading into the *sala* of a San Miguel de Allende home: another of Xavier Barbosa's fortunate finds.

It is intriguing to imagine where Arquitecto Manuel Parra found this quasi-Gothic stone window frame. With his masterly touch, he has placed it beautifully in a house in Mexico City.

Opposite page: Not many people are acquainted with the derelict town of Aduana in the State of Sonora. However, for the intrepid, a visit to this once rich small mining town is very worth while. From the few stone walls left standing, one can imagine what it must have looked like in its heyday when the mine was being worked and there was much liveliness and bustle. This building housed the offices of the mine at the end of the XVII century.

Home of Wolfgang and Gisela Karmeinsky

52

Opposite page: A bare stone wall provides an excellent contrast to the stuccoed masonry walls in this high-ceilinged, elegant living room. In order to prevent crumbling, a sealer must be applied. This also makes it easy to clean and is a slight discouragement to spiders and scorpions from making their homes in the cracks.

Very much at home in Mrs. Havermale's lofty Colonial *sala* is this soft brown *cantera* lamp base depicting St. George on horseback with a rather inoffensive-looking dragon under hoof.

Another living room where decorative architectural details of carved stone enrich the total simplicity of the plaster ceiling and walls. Both the arch in the background and the stone fireplace come from an old and now demolished mansion.

Home of Inez Havermale

Home of Mario González Ulloa Jr.

In the building and decoration of fireplaces, stone is also of great value. Not only does it introduce another color and texture but makes any fireplace, however small, the focal point of any room.

In the living room of Arquitecto Alejandro von Waberer's house, this unusual terra cotta and white fireplace was designed by him around the two primitive stone relief figures which he found in a demolished house.

Making good use of tight corners, both these small bedroom fireplaces with stone cornices and bases are a godsend on cold nights.

Home of Alejandro and Carmen von Waberer

Home of Elton and Martha Hyder

Home of Inez Havermale

Home of Manuel and Teresa Barbachano Ponce

This indoor staircase in the hall of a Spanish Colonial home in the San Angel district of Mexico City is made of dark, highly polished hard stone. The floor in the foreground is paved with 12″ squares of unpolished stone joined very closely.

57

The well-planned, understated simplicity of this exceptional Cuernavaca home is apparent in the dining room. Antiques from the owner's collection are placed here with a fine discrimination. Also interesting is the concept of having two white hexagonal stone dining tables.

The impressive light-colored stone fireplace gives the Barbachano Ponces' *sala* a feeling of grandeur. Above it, a gilt sunburst of wood of magnificent proportions is part of their well-known collection of priceless antiques.

Home of Manuel and Teresa Barbachano Ponce

The city of Puebla must be proud indeed to possess one of the most beautiful of all carved
stone angels. The majestic archangel St. Michael stands on a tall fluted column in the center   61
of the XVIII century fountain that bears his name in the main square of Puebla.

A fine example of the stone carver's art are these delicately carved floral panels at the side of the entrance door of one of the houses in the development of Tetelpa in Mexico City (*opposite*).

The Mexican craftsman infuses the simplest and most utilitarian objects with a certain sense of humor and beauty. The antique stone mill grinds coffee and also corn to make tortillas. The fish is used to sharpen kitchen knives. Many other kitchen objects are also made of this dark *recinto* type of stone. *Molcajetes,* mortars to make chile sauce, the inseparable accompaniment to a good taco and *metates,* native grinders where the cornmeal is made ready for the tortillas, are also made of this same stone.

64

Many varieties of rainspouts, from the plainest to the most extravagant, have been carved throughout the centuries and adorn the façades of Colonial buildings. One of the words used to describe rainspouts in Spanish is *cañón* (cannon) and in several old houses they are indeed made to resemble little cannons with stone or iron wheels on the sides.

Animals are long-time favorites, such as these cats with bells around their necks peering over the street façade of the Hyders' house in San Miguel de Allende.

Rainspouts must be carved from a single piece of stone and when set into the wall, a strong parapet should hold them in place. Since the rainwater of a relatively large roof area is channeled toward them, it emerges with tremendous force. Although now there are more modern ways of solving this problem, architects still use rainspouts to give Colonial type buildings a touch of authenticity.

JOHN BEADLE 79.

BRICK AND MASONRY

IN THE SKILLED HANDS of the Mexican bricklayer even brick, which is considered a rather utilitarian material with not much artistic merit per se, becomes versatile and attractive. Since the advent of reinforced concrete made thinner and lighter walls a possibility, stone and adobe were soon discarded in favor of brick.

It is usually made by hand in little brickyards in areas of the country where good clay is abundant. The making of bricks is truly a family venture, with all the members helping to shape and fire them in primitive ovens. The fortunate results of this individualistic manufacture are that no one brick is exactly like another. To the modern builder this may be annoying, but to those who wish to give their buildings a distinctive feeling, it is a godsend.

Home of Mr. Clifford and Mr. Lindstrom

In the restoration of an old Alamos home, brick has been used throughout. 67
Whitewashed, it makes the spacious outdoor *sala* most attractive.

Home of Josué and Jaqueline Saenz

Undoubtedly one of the great houses of Mexico is the fascinating and most beautiful home of Mr. and Mrs. Josué Saenz in Mexico City.

Home of Josué and Jaqueline Saenz

Not only the house itself but also the setting is pure enchantment. The rambling brick house, built on several levels, overlooks a ravine and is surrounded by extensive grounds with large trees that give it a sense of complete seclusion. Their vast collection of archeology is perhaps one of the most important in the country. With great imagination, the Saenz's have placed the pieces throughout their house in such a way that although one is awed by such magnificence one never has the feeling of being in a museum. This feat has been accomplished partly by combining these treasures with antique furniture of different epochs and styles and by Mrs. Saenz's endearing small bouquets of fresh flowers from her garden. Scattered throughout the house, they give it the warm atmosphere of a much loved home.

Above: Interestingly used brick lines the underside of the stairs that lead to the bedrooms and upper gallery.

Home of Josué and Jaqueline Saenz

The spacious, high-ceilinged gallery, where the largest part of the collection is displayed, can be entered from both an upper and a lower level. Huge wooden beams supported by stone columns open up different areas, giving the house a sense of flowing movement.

Home of Josué and Jaqueline Saenz

Above: A heavy rough wood beam serves both as bookshelf and mantelpiece for this unusual fireplace.

Below: A recessed alcove provides ample space to enjoy the fire and the comfortable cushions placed on the stone hearth make it an inviting nook.

Home of Ramón and Anna Maria Xirau

The simplicity of these four stuccoed and painted brick fireplaces accents the stone decorations to great advantage.

The clean geometric lines of this fireplace are broken only by the brick cornice, molded in the traditional *pecho de paloma* style, and by the little grey stone fruit basket in the center.

Elegantly formal, these recessed bookcases flank the stone fireplace of a *sala* in a San Miguel de Allende home.

Home of Edward and Juliet Yonkers

Basically made of brick, these fireplaces are good illustrations of the versatility of this material and the workmanship of the craftsmen who built them.

Left: Tucked away in the corner of the bedroom, this little charmer was copied from a stone fireplace. The base and the cornice are molded out of brick and the delicately-colored tiles are inspired by XVIII century French faience work and made in the neighboring town of Dolores Hidalgo.

Enchantment radiates from this well-designed alcove in the master bedroom of a house built by Arquitecto Manuel Parra in Mexico City. Above the high, polished wood mantel shelf, three hand-painted Maja plates are set into the wall, giving it a touch of whimsy.

Home of Alfred and Nika Fleissig

Home of Beach and Mane Riley

Simple sculptural form is the keynote of these two stuccoed brick fireplaces in a San Miguel de Allende home. Not perhaps a wise idea, but definitely an attractive one, this fireplace is in the corner of the room of a little boy.

Downstairs, in the *sala* of this same house, the fireplace makes good use of the peculiar contours of the property, which also allows for recessed bookcases.

Here, kitchens are the fortunate possessors of fireplaces, and a cozier idea is hard to imagine.

Left: Much thought has been given by Jean Claire Salsbury, an expert in these matters, to the planning of her seemingly simple kitchen in Cuernavaca. During the warm season the fireplace is used for keeping appliances at hand.

In another kitchen, designed with the functional as well as the esthetic in mind, the arched brick fireplace is not only an attractive feature but a real necessity during the cold winter evenings in Alamos.

Home of Alan and Jean Claire Salsbury

Home of Edward and Catherine Barnes

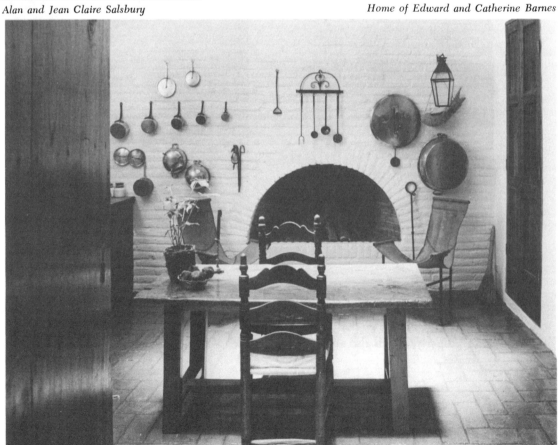

Home of Jorge and Sara Larrea

Home of Bob and Nina Schalkwijk

As an integral and very visible part of the building, chimneys in Mexico also claim the benefit of the craftsman's full attention, as is apparent in these two examples.

Home of Xavier de la Barra

"Club de Vela de la Peña"

Valle de Bravo, a small Colonial village on the shores of an enchanting lake, has become the mecca of the city-weary sportsman. Its natural beauty and its relative nearness to Mexico City make it ideal for this purpose.

On the slopes of a towering crag, *La Peña,* a group of sailing enthusiasts have built a club surrounded by their own attractive weekend houses. Two talented architects, Andrés Casillas and José Yturbe Bernal, arrived in the wake of these nature lovers and are in great part responsible for the fortunate results of this homogeneous community development.

An almost convent-like severity is the recurrent characteristic of this type of architecture. Wood abundant in this region is effectively combined with the roughly stuccoed brick and masonry walls. Touches of color are provided by the rich terra cotta ceramic floor and the deep mustard yellow, woolen rug.

Opposite: The strong, severe lines of the Club de Vela de la Peña are unbroken throughout.

Nothing has been allowed to mar or minimize the architectural concept in any way. This large square window, beveled on one side, allows light to be directed toward the furthest part of the dining room.

Overleaf: All the indoor social and family activities can take place within the four white walls of this light and airy room designed and built by Arquitecto José Yturbe Bernal. By introducing different levels within the same room, he divides the space and gives a dazzling effect of openness within a contained area. Both the back and the armrest of the bench become useful surfaces on which to place small objects and lamps. To this whiteness, color is added by the warm yellow cushions, deep orange rugs and many pots of greenery. The strikingly colorful painting by Pedro Coronel on the back wall gives the last and definite touch.

79

Home of José and Dolores Yturbe

In a more traditional manner, brick is used here to define the free contours of the swimming pool in a most attractive home in San Antonio, Texas. Practically all the decorative building materials, such as carved stone, hand-painted ceramic tiles, floor tiles, ornamental objects and much of the furniture in this house were imported from Mexico. Thanks to the taste of the architect, Don White, these friendly aliens have found a home away from home.

Home of Marshall and Patsy Steves

Many genuine touches, such as the bleached cotton sun umbrella, which is inspired by the ones that shade the fruit stalls in open-air markets in Mexico, give the Steves' house in San Antonio an authentic Mexican flavor.

Home of Marshall and Patsy Steves

In these two charming outdoor areas, brick has been used to great advantage. The floor of the secluded solarium is paved with mellow, thin brick *ladrillo*. Its utter simplicity is greatly enhanced by two rare, carved stone floral urns.

Below: A faithful copy of an old hacienda masonry bench looks very inviting under the pergola of old wooden beams.

Home of Marshall and Patsy Steves

These half-ruined brick arches are the only vestiges of the old tequila hacienda, La Huerta de los Urrea, which once produced the indigenous Mexican drink. They have now become a decorative feature in a large and beautifully kept Alamos garden.

A native of the State of Guerrero painted this lively scene of life in his own village on the wall of the open-air dining room in a country house in Tepoztlán.

Home of Antonio and Francesca Saldivar

Home of Martha Heywood

85

In an often used open-work pattern, these brick lattice screens (*celosías*) have a basic purpose in common to screen or divide an area while allowing the passage of light and air, as in this balustrade and dividing wall on the upper terrace of Eric Noren's home.

Below: This type of *celosía* is used in order to separate the work and storage area from the display section of the store in "Solo con Cita," an elegant new arts and crafts shop in San Miguel de Allende. Since the light here comes only from large windows in the front of the store, the open trellis provides light for the back regions.

Used both indoors and out, *celosías* provide an inexpensive solution to many types of screening or dividing problems.

Home of Beach and Mane Riley

Home of Christopher and Mary King

87

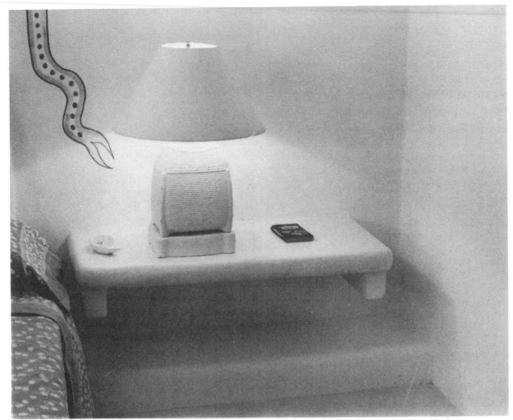

Casa Emilia

Outstanding Mexican architects of today are designing easy care furniture that is integrated with the construction and is built at the same time as the house itself.

White paint is all that is necessary to keep this simple bedroom, designed by **Arquitecto Marco Antonio Aldaco**, in pristine condition. This lasting type of furniture is of great practical value, especially in hot and humid climates where wood must constantly be treated and repainted.

Home of Francisco and Amanda Martinez Negrete

In a more formal contemporary living room, Arquitecto Francisco Martínez Negrete has integrated the sofa and the side table with the corner fireplace. The outstanding virtue of this new type of architectural furniture lies in its uncluttered simplicity.

Below: This elegant sofa has been designed to fit exactly into the alcove formed by the bay window in a living room in Mexico City.

Home of Antonio and Francesca Saldivar

Opposite: Taught to the natives by the Spanish during the time of the colony, the art of making brick vaults has remained until our days one of the most beautiful ways of enclosing space from above. In Xavier Barbosa's perfect dining room, both the vault and ribbing are plastered over and painted white.

Anna María Xirau designed and supervised the construction of this house in the old residential district of San Angel in Mexico City. She has brought her taste and knack for finding treasures in unsuspected places into her home. In the spacious *sala,* the artful combination of antique furniture and modern art has produced excellent results.

Dr. Xirau, a brilliant man of letters, spends much of his time upstairs among the many books and papers, in a general air of warmth and comfort.

Home of Ramón and Anna Maria Xirau

Home of Xavier Barbosa

Home of Robert and Violet Rice

A remarkable example of the vaultmaker's art is this extensive vaulted brick ceiling in the Rices' living room in San Miguel de Allende.

The complicated procedure of building vaults was learned by the natives, whose descendants still profit from this well-taught lesson. The town of Lagos de Moreno, in central Mexico, is one of the few places in the country where the secrets of vault making are passed on from father to son. The Spanish word for vault is *bóveda* and the *bovederos* are a select and much respected clan. *Bóvedas* are built without supporting frames with special smaller size bricks (*cuñas*). It is fascinating to see a vault being built. They are usually started from the four corners and progressively rise from the sides by means of magically accommodating the *cuñas* in the appropriate places until, with a flourish, the last one is inserted which closes the vault in the center.

Home of William and Yolanda Dellekamp

An uncommon ceiling is this almost flat brick vault that rises very gradually from the dentil cornice which surrounds the whole room.

92

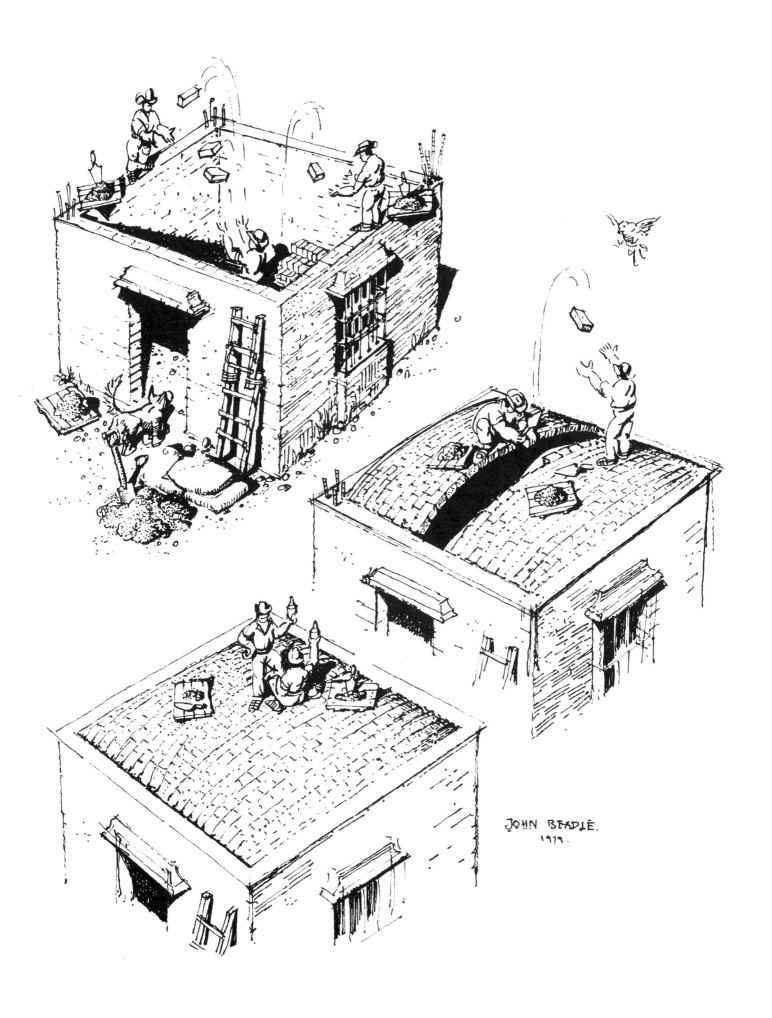

JOHN BEADLE.
1979.

One has only to raise one's eyes to appreciate the skill with which this vaulted
brick ceiling has been built.

The tunnel or barrel vault, which roofs this game room in the old hacienda
of "Ojo Caliente," is called *bóveda de cañon* in Spanish. This type of vaulted   95
ceiling is ideally suited for roofing long and narrow spaces.

96   In strong contrast to the darkly stained stairs, the simple whitewashed brick wall makes a suitably pure background for the innocent communicants in the painting.

Home of Peter and Elisabeth Gerhard

Full of light and a sense of joy, these two bedrooms have also profited from the use of brick, both as a construction and as an ornamental material. In the room above, the big fireplace is stuccoed and whitewashed to match the walls and only the top of the mantelshelf and the frame around the opening is left in natural brick.

Below: Delightful Miss Beatrice Escobedo must be very proud of her bedroom. Here the brick vault is totally integrated with the walls and the whole room is immaculately whitewashed. Color is added by the blue lines on the chest of drawers and the specially woven rug. The bedspread is hand embroidered by the natives of a village near Toluca.

Home of Miguel and Malu Escobedo

Home of Miguel and Malu Escobedo

Home of Miguel and Malu Escobedo

Other rooms in the Escobedos' home are equally successful. Their house is built on a large property in San Jeronimo, on the outskirts of Mexico City. The surrounding garden and large old trees give it an unreal air of enchantment.

The dining room is used in the evenings and on formal occasions. The fascinating object on the ceiling is actually a wool tapestry, the work of Marta Palau. It is placed in this unorthodox fashion to improve the acoustics of the room. How this achieves its objective is difficult to imagine, but the Escobedos are positive in their claim that it works.

Opposite: The sculptural fireplace makes room on both sides for two recessed benches, over which hang sculptures by Helen Escobedo, the owner's talented sister who designed the house.

White corridors around the central patio become ideal places for al fresco meals.

Home of Bob and Nina Schalkwijk

The large and beautifully proportioned *sala* is the soul of the Schalkwijks' house in Mexico City. The double height of the ceiling and the vast window recessed into the far wall give the room airiness and light. Well-seasoned old wood has been used throughout the house. Here, the massive beams and highly waxed floorboards add comforting warmth, complemented by the fine antique furniture, many books and softly glowing Persian rugs.

Casa de las Campanas

The entrance from the street into the elegant Colonial style Casa de las Campanas gives a welcome not only to the visitor but to the tired passerby. Since servants in Mexico take forever to answer the door, even when they have made certain that the caller's business is legitimate by shouting *"quién?"* (who) repeatedly over the intercom and invariably receiving the answer *"yo"* (me), the thoughtfulness of the owner in providing these benches is truly fortunate.

Found in various parts of the country, these brick niches were all designed for religious statues. Although in a sad state, this elaborate example in the corner of a church atrium illustrates the way they were built in Colonial times.

Lower left: A high and narrow niche in the circular brick wall of the stairwell of the Salsburys' home in Cuernavaca makes a stunning showcase for the antique wooden figure of Christ.

Lower right: St. Peter stands clutching his heavenly keys and guarding the entrance to a house in San Miguel de Allende. The thin brick circle above this simple niche was made by a devout mason to keep his patron saint from getting drenched during the rainy season.

Home of Alan and Jean Claire Salsbury

Home of Peter and Patricia Bubela

PLASTER AND STUCCO

PLASTER AND STUCCO as ornamental elements have been used in Mexico since pre-Columbian times. There are still vestiges of stucco work in existence to remind us of what the forebears of the craftsmen of today were capable of creating in this media. Later, the Spanish introduced their own designs, to which the natives added their own fantasy.

Of special interest are the much used *conchas* (shells) which adorn the many embrasured doors and windows of Colonial buildings in Mexico. According to a charming legend, the shell brought blessings to the house because of its association with the pilgrimage to the Shrine of Santiago de Compostela, the center of XVI century religious fervor in Spain. Whether true or not, these graceful ornaments have been, indeed, a blessed gift to the builders of yesterday and today.

AUTHOR'S NOTE: The material I refer to as stucco, from which all the decorations shown in this chapter are molded, is basically a mixture of sand and lime. In Colonial times quick-lime was mixed with the sand. Nowadays, commercially packaged slaked lime is used instead and cement is added to the mixture to prevent crumbling.

Maestro Asunción Escobedo gives the finishing touches to a *concha* in the house that Mr. and Mrs. van der Kemp are restoring in San Miguel de Allende.

Home of Gerald and Florence van der Kemp

As an introduction to the subject of *conchas*, this traditional stuccoed shell over the *sala* door of an original Colonial house in the old Coyoacan district of Mexico City leads us into a veritable treasure trove.

JOHN BEADLE. '79.

Conchas not only serve to decorate embrasured doors and windows, but the imaginative builder finds other interesting ways to use them. With this unusual *concha*, Arquitecto Alejandro von Wuthenau has made this otherwise simple dressing table into the focal point of his daughter's bedroom.

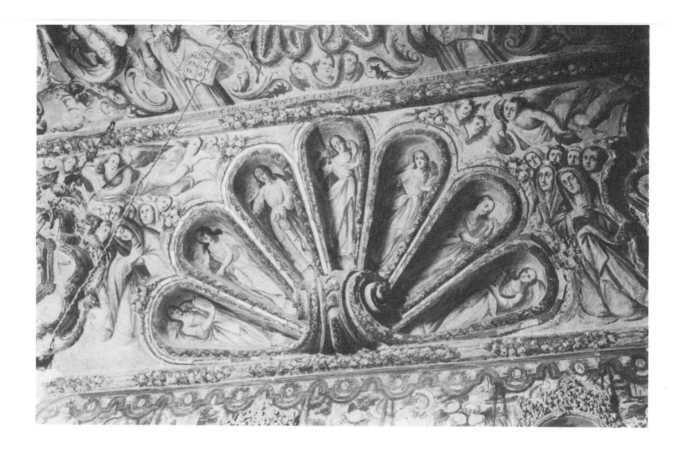

The XVIII century Santuario de Atotonilco, a short distance from San Miguel de Allende, is not only a religious citadel of great importance, but it provides an emotional feeling of spirituality and a constant joy for the senses. Throughout this sanctuary, completed in the desertic countryside in 1748 as a retreat for pilgrims by the venerable and ascetic Padre Alfaro, there is an incredible wealth of artistic expression, which unfortunately is being allowed to fall into complete decay.

The *concha* comes into its own here. Made of stucco or wood and sublimely decorated, gilded and painted, they give an idea of the richness of the native talent harnessed to the Spanish baroque concepts of the XVIII century.

Right: Set into the wall of one of the forgotten side chapels, this large sea conch once served as a holy water stoup.

In the cloister of a beautiful convent which now houses the School of Fine Arts in San Miguel de Allende, this simple *concha* over a stone basin is literally carved out of the thick wall.

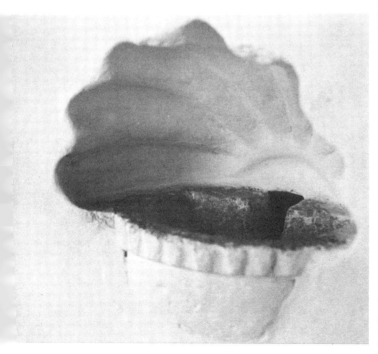

Home of Susie Noel

Many attractive uses are also found for the *concha* when planning bathrooms. Made to fit into the corner of the tiled bathroom at left, the niche makes good use of space which is usually wasted.

In a Cuernavaca home, a large, finely molded concha adds a touch of grace to the semi-circular tiled shower designed by Rodolfo Ayala.

Home of Alexander Kirkland

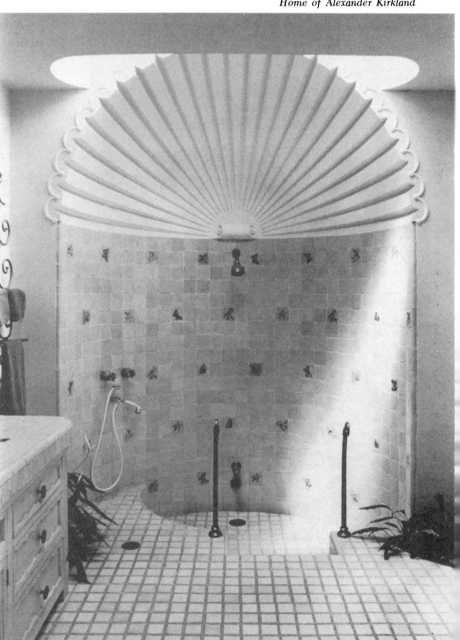

110

A much-favored way of including a *concha* in the bathroom
is to place it over a recessed washbowl.

In Mexico one often discovers art treasures in the most unsuspected places, such as the XVII century Dominican former *convento* of Tlacochahuaya at the end of an unpaved road near the city of Oaxaca.

The small primitive stucco niche at left illustrates the native charm of early Colonial architecture.

The very thick stone walls of some of San Miguel de Allende's Spanish Colonial houses allow depth for these recessed street fountains. The water in this one flows into the square basin from the carved stone spout at the base of the *concha*.

112

Adding interest to the passage between the kitchen and dining room, this fine *concha* is finished off with a delicate spray of leaves molded from the same stucco.

In the distinguished home of the Meisenheimers' in Alamos, Arquitecto René Escobosa designed this beautifully proportioned shell as a headrest in the master bedroom. The lime green cushions over a white woolen bedspread make it both cool and inviting.

Home of Susie Noel

Home of Les Meisenheimer

113

114

Some of the most interesting original *conchas* are to be found in the XVIII century home of the Saldivars'. Great care was taken to preserve their authenticity when the house was being restored; the early painted decorations around the windows were very lightly retouched. Between the two windows stands a rather fierce wooden Santiago in an unusual *nicho de concha,* which has been cut to accommodate his horse's tail.

Home of Antonio and Francesca Saldivar

In a combination rare on the same façade, the intricately worked flower vases (probably a later addition) are made of stucco, while the niche and the columns are made of stone.

An enchanting stucco niche makes a fine setting for this gentle XVIII century polychromed wood madonna.

The flower and acorn motif surrounding the ogee-arched niche suggests a more primitive hand.

117

Still beautiful in spite of its state of decay, this graceful triple *concha* languishes in hopes that some imaginative person will discover it and restore it to its former glory.

Age has given a beautiful patina to this old house in Huejotzingo, and the delicate stucco details give it distinction and a naive charm. The graceful old grille over the window must be the envy of many a collector, since these grilles with lead castings are almost impossible to find nowadays.

119

Both indoors and out, stucco has long been used in Mexico to plaster walls and to mold the many features that so enhance windows, doors, street signs and cornices. This small selection has been carefully chosen from different parts of the country.

On one side of the newly remodelled "Teatro Principal" in Puebla, this oval street sign in white stucco against a pale yellow wall is a great improvement on the usual variety.

Windows facing the street in Mexico City, Alamos and Cuernavaca show how the imagination of the native craftsman can make out of the most ordinary window an indigenous feature of the façade.

The façade of the XVI century primitive church in Izamal, a small village in Yucatán, is roughly plastered with stucco and painted yellow and white. A distinctly whimsical feature is the iron balcony that keeps the priest from falling down when he sets the church clock.

121

Home of Dr. David Brucilovsky

Small cupolas built of brick and mortar and decorated with stucco molding embellish many of the houses built in Colonial style. Not only are they gratifying to look at, but they are an often necessary extra source of light. These two cupolas are both outstanding features of the dining rooms of two San Miguel de Allende homes (*above and right*).

122

The sculptural effect of the exclusive resort hotel, Las Hadas, is partly due to the many fantastically shaped domes.

The use of stucco in pre-Columbian times is well exemplified by this most extraordinary Mayan mask discovered in Kohunlich in the State of Quintana Roo.

Painted the same mellow apricot color as the wall, this stucco San Miguel archangel bravely challenges the visitor who enters Federico Siller's charming weekend retreat.

Home of Federico Siller

High on a street wall in San Angel, this carved stone medallion is set into a terra cotta colored wall decorated with a stucco hexagonal pattern.

Home of Jorge and Sara Larrea

A lovely stucco medallion depicting the Christ child as the Good Shepherd has been molded over the stone frame at the entrance of the Instituto de Bellas Artes in Puebla.

126

Home of Rafael and Enriqueta Casasola

Straw mats laid over the wooden forms used to hold the freshly poured concrete while it set give this ceiling in Cuernavaca its interesting pattern.

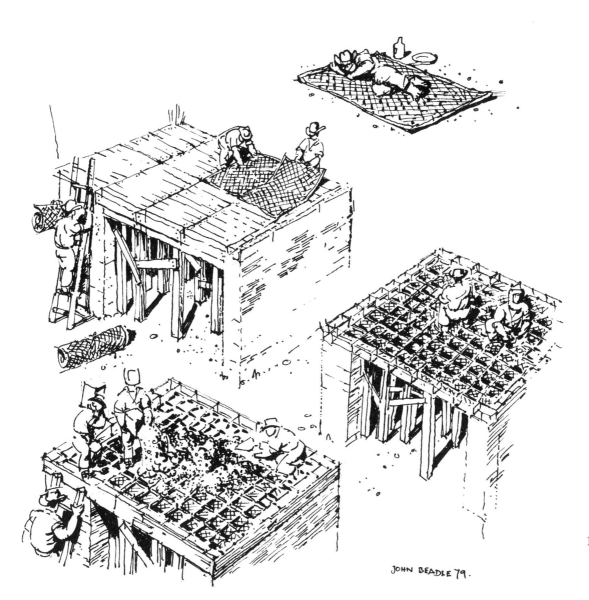

JOHN BEADLE 79.

128   Mrs. Havermale's kitchen door is well guarded by this canine giant and surrounded by a simple stucco frame surmounted by an intricately worked leaf motif.

Entering from the higher level, the elegance of this unique entrance hall can
be appreciated from another angle. The white sections of the vault allow light
to pass behind them and fall on the roughly stuccoed oxidized deep yellow wall.

Although the interior walls of this house are only 6″ thick the niches in the bedroom suggest that they are much thicker. The depth of the fireplace gives room on either side for cabinets and bookshelves. The stucco molding adds a touch of lightness.

Two tall stucco native versions of Corinthian columns painted a deep Pompeiian red stand at the entrance to the living room of Ronald Thomae's home in San Miguel de Allende.

131

132   Not only is a wood-burning fireplace an ornament in any room, but it also provides the most romantic source of heat. Facing the bed, this corner fireplace is charmingly decorated with a touching miniature hunting scene.

This unusual rounded fireplace gives the effect of sculptural plasticity. Through a glass-covered opening in the ceiling above, daylight bathes it in a delicate glow. The owner and designer of the house painted the small oval fresco over the cornice, the only touch of color in the unrelieved whiteness of the room.

Two *nichos de concha* flank this simple fireplace in the great bedroom of a house in San Miguel de Allende.

Home of Susie Noel

Home of Alejandro and Carmen von Waberer

Home of Susie Noel

With an adventurous eye for color, Mrs. Noel has chosen bedspreads in shades of dark blue, hot pink and orange, which add warmth and gaiety to the otherwise sober room. The white fluted semi-circular fireplace in the library stands out from the lime green walls. The backs of the niches are painted a deep pink against which the priceless rose Wedgewood porcelain glimmers softly. The material that covers the chairs has also been chosen with a keen appreciation for design and color.

In an upstairs bedroom, the hearth extends on both sides of the fireplace to form a useful bedside shelf.

This unusually shaped fireplace is topped by a large stucco *piña*. Pineapples, an old symbol of hospitality, are dearly cherished sources of inspiration for the craftsmen of Mexico, who use this delightful fruit to beautify many wood, brass and stone ornamental objects.

The space on both sides of this bedroom fireplace has been used to great advantage. Two arched niches with open shelves add valuable storage space to the room. The recessed door completes the illusion that the walls are very thick.

The classical fluting of the hood over the stove and the arch under it give this most agreeable tiled kitchen a feeling of being part of an old hacienda.

WOOD

THE TRADITION OF excellence imparted by the Spanish artists of the XVI, XVII and XVIII centuries to the native woodcarvers has produced most fortunate results, which can still be appreciated today. These colonizers introduced the craftsmen not only to iron woodcarving tools, but to the lofty art concepts of Europe of that time. The carving of wood vied with ornamental stone in giving great buildings wealth and importance. Nowadays, following this tradition, doors, windows, and many other architectural and decorative elements are still painstakingly and skillfully carved by their descendents, such as Maestro Cruz Caballero, of well-deserved fame in San Miguel de Allende.

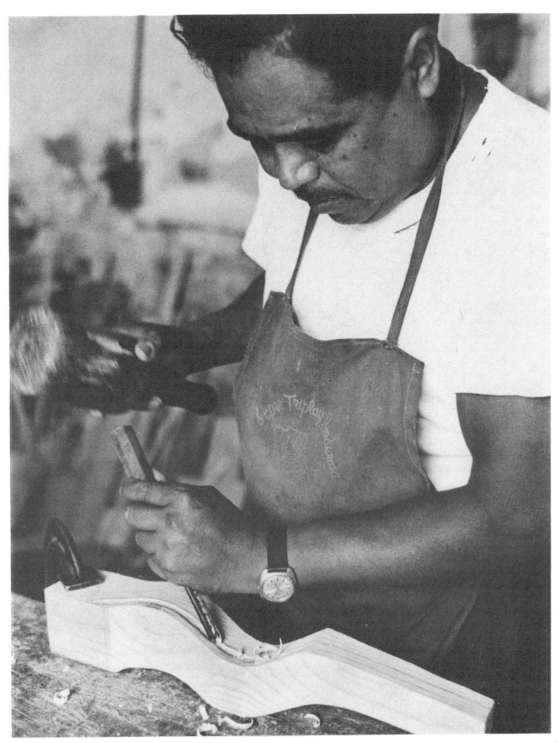

Villa Alejandra

Wood, one of the most precious of nature's offerings, is transformed into art
by the skill and imagination of man. Antiqued in a faded olive green, this
extraordinary door leads the privileged guest into a palm-surrounded retreat in
the Villa Alejandra in Acapulco.

139

Two richly carved doors painted in dark green and red tones bring their own unparalleled grace into the Moorish style of this guest house. Two *santos* painted on tin are set into the carved design of one of the doors, which adds a further touch of glowing color.

Villa Alejandra

Opposite: Delicate as lace, this ethereal wooden gate subtly divides the indoor from the outdoor regions in the Saenz's home. The slender turned bars can compete with ironwork in finesse of workmanship.

Home of Josué and Jaqueline Saenz

Home of Josué and Jaqueline Saenz

Massiveness is the keynote of these two doors. The upper rough primitive gate was made to resist the temptation to escape from a *convento* cell or perhaps from prison. In small country towns, these strong wooden gates are still used to lock up prisoners. Sometimes hands emerge from the square openings asking the passerby for a cigarette.

The entrance door also had to be impregnable. This pair of carved doors, which must once have belonged to a small village church, now serves as the front door of the Saenz's house.

Home of Josué and Jaqueline Saenz

Inspired by the antique cupboards found in the old houses in San Cristobal de las Casas near the Guatemalan border, this high narrow door has been fashioned with a shell at each end. This design is easily adaptable to contemporary or Mediterranean types of architecture.

Esc. 1:10

143

Opposite and above: The art of woodcarving finds its greatest expression in this tall and stately entrance door of a house in Querétaro. Baroque leaf-eating human heads taper into intricate scrolls surrounding a scalloped shell. A life-like larger shell surmounts the lower panels, which are usually open to admit people into the house. In the center of this lower panel, a pair of carved Indian heads are perhaps a cry for recognition of the native craftsmen who carved this marvel. Great bronze-studded nails are placed throughout the doors in an almost geometric design.

Simplicity indeed becomes elegance when this weathered old door is set into the embrasured entrance of a house in Cuernavaca. The combination of the sun-bleached whitish tones of the door and the warm patina of the color-streaked walls delight the passerby.

This carved lower section of a 15′ high door in the church of the little mining town of Mineral de Cata, a short distance from Guanajuato, can easily be copied to make a wonderful entrance door for a Colonial style house. The transom should be cut in order to meet the design at the top. To achieve the full depth of the carving, at least 4″ very dry wood should be used.

Surrounded by a simple stone arch, this door is another example of the skilled workmanship of the past. Made of dark hardwood, it has withstood the ravages of time and weather. The geometric division of the panels and the wide molding in no way detract from the exquisiteness of the fine carving.

Home of Dr. Mario González Ulloa

The great fondness the Mexican craftsman has for angels would not be completely expressed if he could not also endow them with life in wood. On this pair of baroque doors, angels of all sizes cavort among the fruits and greenery, charmingly reminiscent of a child's puzzle where the number of angels must be guessed correctly.

Below: It is still possible today to find excellent woodcarvers to interpret contemporary or earlier designs in the many kinds of wood available in Mexico. These doors were carved for Mr. Wilson's studio by a local carpenter in San Miguel de Allende.

Home of David and Anne Wilson

Left: In a naive and more primitive manner, two little angels draw back wooden draperies to disclose a huge, flower-shaped opening in this unusual front door of an Alamos home. *Arquitecto* René Escobosa, with great ingenuity, added the narrow iron bars above and below the door to give it the right measurements.

Home of Russell Hurd

Refreshingly white, these two entrance doors in two seaside resorts also draw attention to the skill of the modern woodcarver. These doors with a tropical motif give access to Mr. Hurd's charming *sala* in Acapulco.

Right: The finely featured faces and the stylized fruit on the diamond-shaped panels of the small arched door add yet another Mediterranean touch to the Hotel Las Hadas.

Intricately carved, these geometric panels are polished to give them a diamond-like quality. The greatly favored *piña* suitably makes its appearance in these perfectly finished kitchen cabinets.

Home of Tirey Ford

Home of Josué and Jaqueline Saenz

Opposite: There is a Spanish saying: "*Un santo triste es un triste santo.*" (A sad saint is not much of a saint.) Here, these primitive little *santos* carved on the antiqued white door panels of the Steves' recreation room cupboards look happy in their saintly way.

Home of Marshall and Patsy Steves

Above: Nothing delights the architect more than to have the furniture and decoration of the house chosen to complement his architectural concept. In this thoroughly well planned and furnished house, the admirably carved antique composite *ropero* (cupboard) truly fullfils this role.

151

In great contrast to the pervading light contemporary atmosphere of an elegant room, this travelling desk of a Spanish *señor* strikes a strong and serious note in an otherwise fanciful and relaxed ambiance.

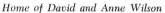
Home of David and Anne Wilson

Home of Karl Eric Noren

In a completely different and feminine setting, the light Victorian writing table and chair make good use of the well-lit corner of the bedroom.

The grape and wheat motif of the brass candlesticks indicate their religious provenance, since these well-known symbols represent the sacramental bread and wine.

Home of Rufino and Olga Tamayo

Home of Herrick and Elisabeth Nuzom

Complete opposites to their counterparts on the preceding pages, these rustic pieces, thought fit only for a farm kitchen, now appear in two elegant entrance halls. In the Nuzoms' narrow *zaguán*, the plain shelf is the only thing allowed to break the simplicity of the whitewashed walls.

Standing against the roughly stuccoed wall, the bleached, scrubbed pine *trastero* (kitchen dresser) holds an amusing assortment of objects, including the photograph of the owner of the house at work.

153

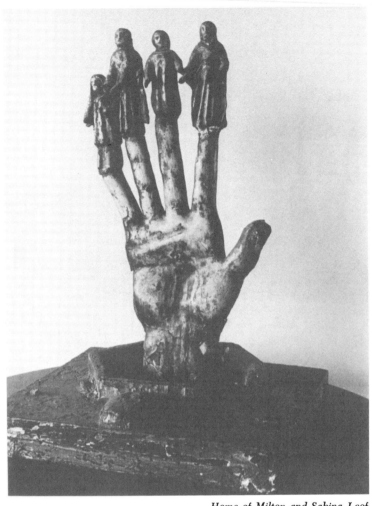

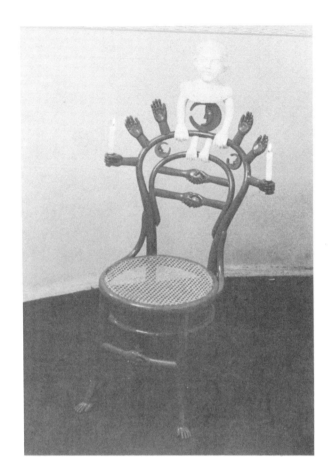

Home of Milton and Sabina Leof

Extremely rare, and probably dating from the XVII century, is this pierced, bleeding hand of Christ, with himself, the Virgin Mary, St. Joseph and the Virgin's parents growing out of the fingers.

Above and below: On the other and profane hand, the talented and versatile Pedro Friedeberg has become the well-known master of the art of the chair. Hands, feet and butterflies, singly and in myriad combinations and colors, are a seductive invitation to the posteriors of humans, sub-humans and to the enchanting denizens of his own imagined fairyland.

Home of Pedro Friedeberg

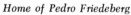

154

Hotel La Mansion Galindo

Xavier Barbosa's wit as well as his talent for finding the impossible is apparent here. These antique polychromed woodcarvings of Adam and Eve discreetly indicate to the visitor of the "Hotel La Mansión Galindo" where these most necessary places are to be found.

One of the many Colonial treasures in the Barbachano's collection is this intricately carved hardwood chest. The delicate monstrance in the center panel indicates that it might have been made to store religious vestments in the sacristy of a church.

Home of Manuel and Teresa Barbachano Ponce

155

Home of Wolfgang and Gisela Karmeinsky

Home of Ignacio and Guadalupe Iturbe

Home of Alexander Kirkland

Right: The exact contours of this finely worked wrought iron lock have been followed by a wooden molding which ends in a spray of leaves. The patina of age has given the surface of this beautiful antique chest a sensual feeling.

Upper left: Recessed into the wall of a child's room, this fairytale dark green and red painted toy cabinet shares the German aspect of the pet animals it supports.

A kind Spanish tradition makes the placing of a bench at the entrance to a house an indispensable courtesy. Here, in the hall of Mr. Kirkland's Cuernavaca home, this carved dark wood bench with its long, comfortable cushion makes waiting decidedly more pleasant.

156

No saint has captured the imagination of the popular craftsman more than *Santiago* (St. James). The first Apostle to become a martyr, his body was miraculously transported to Spain and, according to legend, rests in the Shrine of Santiago de Compostela. An exceptional rendering of this much revered saint stands here on an early XIX century Mexican Chippendale style table.

157

Home of the Marquis and Marquise de la Rozière

Four enchanting wood ornaments which are
small masterpieces of their kind.
Above: This XVIII century French flower basket is so beautifully carved and polished that
it gives more the feeling of having been made
out of stone than of wood.

Home of Dr. Mario González Ulloa

Home of Karl Eric Noren

Home of Beach and Mane Riley

Home of Manuel and Teresa Barbachano Ponce

The dream of a Mexican child is centered on the Three Wise Men. According to an old Spanish tradition, they bring good children presents on January 6th. Every year this colorful wooden trio is placed near the nativity crèche by anxious little hands.

The Barbachanos are indeed fortunate to possess this remarkably carved polychromed panel. Gold has been worked into the somber red, green and blue of the robe to give it the burnished and glowing appearance commonly found in this type of Colonial wood carving.

Opposite: An intricately carved and gilded jar bearing a tall, flowery bouquet, probably once graced an altar in a Colonial church.

Traditionally, ornamental angels perform varied services in the decoration of a home. One such serves as a lamp base. Yet another simply provides joy.

159

Home of Manuel and Teresa Barbachano Ponce

Opposite: Pensive and *simpático* is this wood patron saint of the garden. It is the distinctive work of artist Jean Byron Fernández, who is responsible not only for this sculpture but for many of the original light fixtures and other decorative objects in this San Antonio, Texas home.

The decorative process known as *estofado*, from the French *etoffe* (cloth), has skillfully been applied to this small Colonial wood figure. This method consists of stuccoing and then completely gilding the statue. The colors are then applied and lastly the design is sharply incised with a *grafio* into the overlaying layers of color. This allows the gold to emerge and give its glitter to those areas chosen by the artist.

Hand raised in blessing, this benign carved wood bust of God the Father watches over the Hyders' library. In pre-revolution times, it was probably placed on the highest part of the main altar of a small country church, where similar figures are sometimes found.

Casa de las Campanas

Home of Elton and Martha Hyder

161

Home of Milton and Sabina Leof

Carved out of hard pine, this Mexican provincial adaptation of a Victorian sofa was made in Chiapas. The softly glowing waxed finish of the wood is subtly complemented by the comfortable cushions made of an antique oriental rug in faded rose tones. Behind the sofa lies an inscrutable Chinese-looking Colonial wood lion which the Leofs discovered in Puebla. Above it all hangs the serene portrait of a little boy painted by well-known XIX century painter José María Estrada.

A narrow balcony enclosed by a finely turned wooden balustrade divides the height of the lofty dining room in the Saldivars' home. It can be used as a minstrel gallery or for a string quartet during their elegant dinner parties.

Home of Antonio and Francesca Saldivar

163

Home of Christopher and Mary King

In an exceptional and attractive manner, *Arquitecto* Manuel Parra has divided the ceiling of an asymmetrical living room in a house in Mexico City. By resting massive beams on simple tall grey stone pillars, he achieves a feeling of unrestrained spaciousness.

Home of José and Dolores Iturbe

Great ingenuity has been used to find this way of allowing air to circulate through the rooms of weekend houses in damp Valle de Bravo without leaving the house open to intruders.

An extremely simple glass and wood separation serves as both door and window in a contemporary house in Valle de Bravo.

Home of José and Dolores Iturbe

165

Home of Rufino and Olga Tamayo

Home of Helen Henley

This black-specked cobalt blue jaguar tamely guards the staircase in the Tamayo's house in Mexico City. This type of wooden animal, painted in vibrant colors, is carved by the natives of a region near San Cristobal de las Casas.

Above and below: Disporting themselves on the lawn of a garden in Cuernavaca are these two faded antique wooden animals. The sheep was probably part of a nativity scene or the *"Agnus Dei"* (Lamb of God) of an old church.

Every feather is painstakingly painted in black and white on this pair of happy clucking hens. They are the work of native craftsmen from a village near Cuernavaca.

Home of Stewart and Alys Cort

Home of Helen Henley

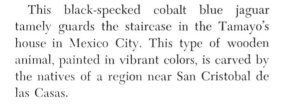

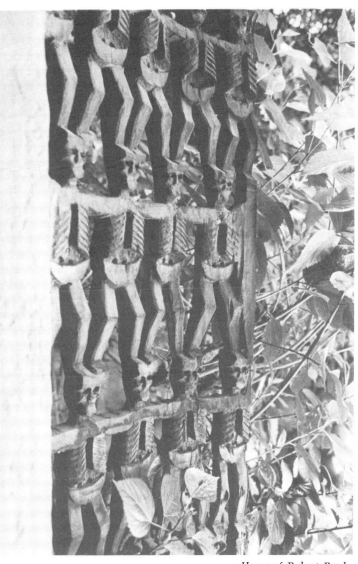

Typifying the Mexican fixation on death, this interesting primitive wood sculpture by Maximo Ibarra has been used by Mr. Brady as a screen in the garden of his Cuernavaca home.

Home of Robert Brady

Home of Rufino and Olga Tamayo

A painted wood bust of Señora Tamayo is placed in a niche in the entrance hall of their home. The large *batea* below is carved from a single piece of wood and highly polished.

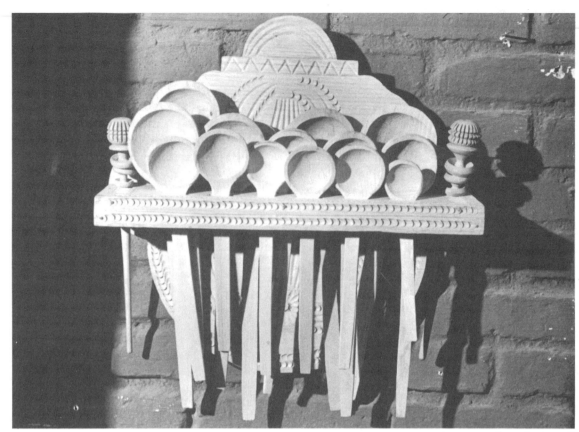

From the hands of very primitive native craftsmen come these simple wood domestic objects. The kitchen spoon rack can be found in any market in the State of Michoacan, and the most elaborately carved are found in the Patzcuaro open-air market on Fridays. The one shown here was photographed in the "Artes Populares de Tequis" shop on the main square in San Miguel de Allende.

Below: The *vara* furniture is made in Alamos in the State of Sonora out of twigs that are specially cut to support the tomatoes and grape vines grown in the neighboring regions. Twig cutting and collecting, and mailing jumping beans to foreign countries, seem to be favorite occupations of this town. The packages containing the very active beans enliven the post office with their antics.

These same twigs are used in making the *vara* ceilings for which Alamos is famous.

168

Wood is very much in evidence in the houses of Temascaltepec and Valle de Bravo, since these two old towns are surrounded by extensive forests.

The railing of the double staircase that joins two balconies on the facade of a Temascaltepec townhouse is made of simply cut straight wood bars.

Wood used outdoors in these regions is protected by coating it with tar dissolved in kerosene, which gives it its rich dark color.

Simple wide boards prop up the beamed overhanging roof of a Valle de Bravo weekend home.

The long narrow window is shut off by a railing made of vertical narrow slats.

Home of Jesús and Yolanda Morales Saviñon

Home of David and Anne Wilson

Home of Jorge and Sara Larrea

The constant preoccupation of the builders and architects of Mexico has been to make ceilings as attractive as possible. In Colonial times, or in houses that are now built in Colonial style, this has been achieved by the use of wooden beams, giving the craftsman and the designer a large field in which to exercise their imagination.

Elaborately carved wood or stone corbels are often placed at each end of the beam, providing both added strength and elegance.

Hotel La Mansión Galindo

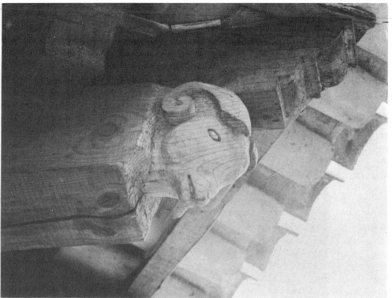

A delightful primitive ram's head (*above*) makes a fitting end for this huge master beam and also for this chapter.

Nicholas Schlee, the talented designer of this house, has introduced into it many of the traditional features of the Tarascan Indians' homes. The covered area which partly surrounds the house greatly enlarges the living space by adding a well-proportioned outdoor living room.

The wood pillars used here to support the beams of the over-hanging roof were carved with their sacred symbols of the sun and the moon by Tarascan Indians.

Home of Oliver and Estelle Clapp

Home of Oliver and Estelle Clapp

CHAPTER VI

TERRA-COTTA AND TILES

TERRA-COTTA, in Italian, means baked earth. From this fascinating material, with its long association with antiquity and great civilizations of the past, many basic architectural and decorative objects are still being made and used in today's building.

One of the mainstays of the many indigenous cultures of Mexico, its use goes back 5,000 years or more. Terra-cotta is also one of the mainstays of building in this country today. Floor tiles, *losetas,* curved roof tiles, *tejas,* balusters, rainspouts and the infinite variety of flowerpots that embellish every patio are made of this warm brownish-red material.

The use and manufacture of glazed tiles, *azulejos,* from the Arabic *al-zulaich* (little stone), is another of the precious gifts imparted by the Spanish colonizers to the craftsmen of Mexico. The method employed in the fabrication of these tiles was imported from the town of Talavera de la Reina in Spain, where the practice of mixing a glaze containing an oxide of tin which prevents the colors from running into each other when the tiles are fired made it possible to have a perfectly outlined design.

The two centers of this craft in Mexico are Puebla, where the well-known blue and white Talavera pottery is made, and Dolores Hidalgo, where tile making has become the largest industry. Four basic colors are used in the decoration of this type of tiles: cobalt blue, emerald green, terra-cotta red and chrome yellow. The surface over which the designs are painted is oyster white and black is used to outline the design.

Because of its excellent thermic qualities, tile has long been used to face cupolas. The maestro and his assistant here are laying an interesting blue and white pattern over a small cupola in the Van Der Kemps' house.

Home of Gerald and Florence van der Kemp

The startling combination of the blue and white tiled columns against the yellow, blue and terra-cotta facing of the walls make San Francisco Acatepec, a small church near Puebla, an undoubted masterpiece of the baroque in Mexico.

175

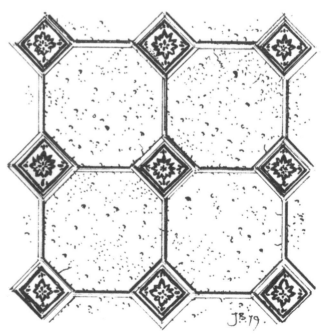

Opposite and right: The fascinating tradition of facing the street walls of houses with interspaced glazed and unglazed tiles makes walking on the streets of Puebla a delight.

Tiles in all shapes, sizes and colors in innumerable combinations and patterns make this beautiful city unique.

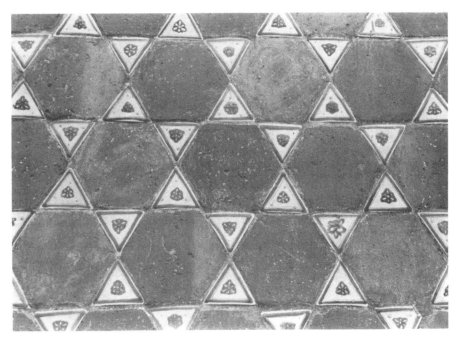

The very long façade of the *Casa de los Muñecos* (House of the Dolls) on a small street near the center of Puebla is an incredible mixture of stucco, tile and ironwork that, in spite of its overdecoration, has a rather delightful and impressive appearance. It is easy to imagine a rococo confectioner applying the white stucco of the cornice with a gigantic frosting tube over and over until all the caryatids and convolutions are finished to meet the demands of his fancy. The tile pictures are life-size and very beautiful. The figures and animals are formed by large glazed tiles surrounded by terra-cotta squares.

The masterpiece of the frosting style of architectural decoration is certainly the Casa del Alfeñique in Puebla. The street façade is literally dripping with this sugary-looking stucco. *Alfeñique* is, in fact, a sugar paste with which confectioners in Mexico mold all sorts of animals, coffins and little dishes with the best offerings of the Mexican cuisine to sell in the streets and markets on the Day of the Dead. Built for the sum of 14,900 Pesos at the end of the XVIII century by José de María Ychauregay as a private residence, it is now a museum.

The cobalt blue and off-white glazed tiles set into the terra-cotta hexagonal *losetas* wink like stars against the pale blue of the patio walls.

Surrounding the *zaguán* (entrance hall) of the XVII century former *convento* de Santa Rosa, now the Museum of Popular Art of the State of Puebla, is this tiled dado of fine antique Puebla tiles with the black and white cross of St. Dominic in the center.

In the now austerely paved patio of this same building, the central stone fountain is also faced with XVII century tiles which have preserved their color to perfection.

This light blue heron and wooly white sheep, which form part of the tiled façade of the church of San Francisco Acatepec, could be reproduced nowadays in the Uriarte tile factory in Puebla and used to decorate a kitchen or a fireplace. The cobalt blue and off-white garland below these animals would make a stunning edging for a terra-cotta floor.

The numerals of this striking clock, set atop the bell tower of the former *convento* de Santa Rosa de Viterbo in Querétaro, are rounded, glazed, oyster-white tiles with the numbers painted in black.

Both tasteful and endearing are the oval glazed plaques placed on the tombs of the faithful in the church of Santa Maria Tonanzintla, a short distance from Puebla.

Fabrica de Azulejos Uriarte

One of the oldest tile and Talavera ware factories in Puebla is owned by the Uriarte family. On the walls of their sunny yellow patio they display several pictures made of multicolored glazed tile to tempt those who are in the process of decorating their homes.

Both the costumed, fairytale extravaganza and the brownish-grey art nouveau snails performing a glissando on an ochre background dome form this amusing and revealing sampler.

Whimsically cross-eyed, this angel is an example of the many glazed tile pictures on religious subjects that adorn the façades of many of the churches in Puebla.

Nowhere does the glazed and decorative tile have more preponderance than in the kitchen. In this respect, the cavernous kitchen of the former *Convento* de Santa Rosa in Puebla is unsurpassed. Walls, ceiling and floor are smothered in small glazed squares. A great effort has been made to keep it looking exactly as it was in the days when the good sisters, led by the cooking genius of the age, Sor Andrea de la Asunción, prepared the famous *molé poblano* for the first time. This chocolate and ground chile sauce soon became the *ne plus ultra* of the Mexican cuisine.

In a humbler way, the kitchen of the XVII century former *Convento* of Santa Mónica also exemplifies the way of life of the nuns who lived here undiscovered for many years, hiding from religious persecution. This magnificent former *convento* has now become the State Museum for Religious Art.

Two excellent *costumbrista* paintings of the 1800's illustrate the culinary customs of XIX century Mexico. They also give us a glimpse into the interior of the kitchen and dining room of a hacienda.

Below: Molé poblano is in the process of being made here. The artist's concern with showing the difference in the existing social classes is always apparent in his paintings. The ingredients for the *molé* are set out on the table, including the unfortunate turkey. The servants are at work, while an old crone whispers a love message she has been paid to deliver, into the apparently uninterested ear of the *señorita* of the house.

185

The combination of wood and tile gives this recessed stove an old-world feeling. Terracotta and off-white *azulejos* face the walls of the alcove, and the ample space on both sides of the burners allows for spices and other condiments to be at hand.

Below: David Newman designed and built this attractive and efficient kitchen, where he can exercise his talent as a gourmet cook. He combined reddish-brown and off-white Dolores ceramic tile with a harder machine-made variety. This provides firmer edges for the working counters and a smoother surface for the table in the foreground.

Home of David and Mary Newman

Home of Alexander Kirkland

Two black-haired children smilingly offer a bowl of fruit and a legend: *"Mi amor contigo Pan y Cebolla."* (With you, my love, I could survive on bread and onions.)

The result achieved by framing the kitchen window in the Nuzom house in Alamos with blue and white *medio paño* tiles is both original and attractive. The wide-tiled central island makes an excellent work area and adds a useful extra sink.

Home of Herrick and Elisabeth Nuzom

Terra-cotta and off-white glazed ceramic tiles line the alcove of the barbecue grill in a San Antonio, Texas, home. These tiles from Dolores Hidalgo are now available in many cities of the southwestern United States.

187

A fascinating medley of designs and colors makes the *brasero* in the Wolgins' Cuernavaca kitchen look both unique and authentic. The tiled shelf under this stove is a good place to keep their native pottery.

Home of Jack and Muriel Wolgin

Home of David and Mary Newman

Lined inside with the same tiles as the walls, the dark green-edged case for cookbooks is a practical feature for any tiled kitchen.

Home of Rufino and Olga Tamayo

Pottery is another craft in which the Mexicans excel. These simple cream-colored Tzintzuntzán plates with native scenes drawn in black are displayed between green and red ceramic slices of watermelon.

A recessed, rose-colored niche, which displays a collection of archeological objects, antique Talavera ware and well-chosen old Puebla pottery, becomes a living page from the history of Mexico.

From the Fourniers' collection of beautiful old ceramics, these three reddish-brown and olive green painted bowls illustrate the best of the old Guanajuato ceramic ware.

Home of Raoul and Carolina Fournier

Home of Rufino and Olga Tamayo

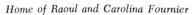

189

Home of Marshall and Patsy Steves

The lively yellow of these simple niches makes a perfect background for the vivid pinks, 191 blues and greens of the many objects of Mexican popular art that Mrs. Steves collects.

Similar to the earliest flooring material in Colonial buildings are these square, unglazed, terra-cotta *cuarterones*, which have been used to tile the outdoor *sala* and a small dining area in two Mexican style houses in San Antonio, Texas.

Home of Marshall and Patsy Steves

To display part of his extensive collection of archeological figures, Rufino Tamayo has made excellent use of the stair landing. The age encrusted reddish-brown terra-cottas look splendid against a blue background that could only have been mixed on the master's palette.

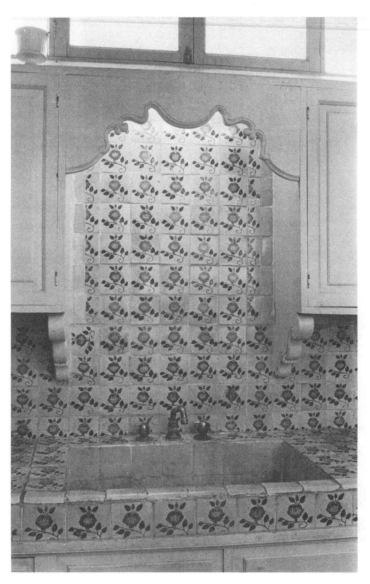

Opposite page: The earliest function given to glazed tile in the times of the Spanish colony was to line bathtubs and to tile the wall surfaces that surrounded washbowls in *convento* refectories and grand dining rooms. In the *Casa del Alfeñique* the niche has been inlaid with blue and white *medio-paño* tiles.

The antique water jug and bowl are made of original XVIII century Talavera of Puebla. *Below:* This yellow and green tiled double tub in a small outdoor courtyard of a Colonial former *convento* in Querétaro was probably considered by the hardy friars a suitable place in which to discuss the daily affairs of the community while engaging in the dangerous pastime of bathing.

Pink thistles, a very old design from Puebla, give freshness to a small kitchen in San Miguel de Allende.

In a contemporary surrounding, off-white glazed tiles with a touch of cobalt blue face the walls and line the stone bathtub of this elegant bathroom.

Home of David and Anne Wilson

Home of David and Anne Wilson

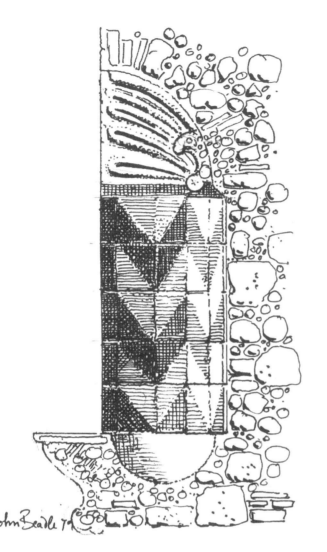

195

Home of Susie Noel

Blue and off-white Greco-Roman figures and an edging of the same colors give this tiled tub an echo of the Mediterranean.

Home of Oliver and Estelle Clapp

Unusual and subtly colored, these sculptural tiles depicting a variety of animals were specially designed and made for the Clapps' home by Nicolas Schlee.

Like old cards from a child's game, these multicolored Puebla tiles give the street wall a joyous and *simpático* touch.

A collection of old Spanish street numbers and letters becomes an imaginative ornament for this simple fireplace.

Original in concept and design, these tin-framed tile wall plaques made in the Marfil workshop of Jean Byron Fernández are also used as ashtrays.

"Artes Populares de Tequis"

Home of Alexander Kirkland

197

Home of Pedro and Virginia Aspe

One of the outstanding landmarks in the romantic cobblestone-paved district of San Angel in Mexico City is the imposing terra-cotta colored and vine-covered house of the Aspes'. An unglazed ceramic balustrade serves as a parapet and gives the house a distinct Italian character.

JOHN BEADLE.
79.

Curved roof tiles, *tejas*, are still found on houses of many small towns in Mexico. As these *tejas* get older and rain falls on them, they acquire a lovely greenish-black patina. Thankfully, they have not yet been superseded by the unattractive asbestos or corrugated tin roofing.

Below: Made out of the same curved roof tiles cut in half, is this *celosía de media teja* (lattice screen made with roof tiles cut in half) that partly encloses the laundry area of a house in Tepoztlan.

Home of Peter and Elisabeth Gerhard

Home of Edward and Juliet Yonkers

In a vegetable garden, roof tiles are also ingeniously used to make this flower-like lettuce bed. It looks pretty and discourages snails from creeping up and eating the young plants.

Below: In order to keep moisture from evaporating and to make tending the plants easier, square *cuarterones* are loosely placed in rows between the young corn in a vegetable garden in Alamos.

Home of Edward and Catherine Barnes

201

CHAPTER VII

IRON, METAL AND GLASS

IRON WAS UNKNOWN in Mexico before the Spanish conquest. This, in fact, had almost fatal consequences for Hernan Cortez and his men, who had to resort to shoeing their horses with silver and to repairing their weapons with copper, since Mexico was rich in both these metals at that time.

At first, iron was used for military purposes. However, when peace was restored and the Spanish began to build houses and religious edifices, necessary objects such as locks, bolts and hinges were made of iron. As time went by, more elaborately worked grilles and railings were added.

Spain kept a jealous eye on the working of iron in the New World, and at one time even prevented the mining of iron ore. Iron was then unnecessarily imported from Spain at a fantastic cost and with much travail. In spite of these difficulties and the stringent rules of the existing guilds of blacksmiths in Mexico, Spanish monks taught this craft to the natives, who soon learned to work the metal and gave it the stamp of their own creative fantasy.

Brass, copper and tin have become an integral part of the crafts which are practiced in Mexico today. To these metals, the present-day craftsmen also give their own personal stamp. Maestro Sergio Trejo, with great ability, gives the finishing touches to a brass star-shaped light fixture.

"Platería Trejo"

202

An excellent example of XIX century ironwork is the balcony of a house in Puebla. The basic iron design has been embellished with finely wrought brass and copper leaves and flowers.

Three wrought iron railings of the late Colonial period show the use of brackets, which added strength to the long sections and incidentally gave them a further decorative touch.

In the Casa del Alfeñique in Puebla, they were also used for hanging bird cages in the patio.

204

Ironwork in Alamos has a special character of its own. The many window railings are almost always finished on top with this design.

Looking through the simple iron gates, it is easy to catch a glimpse of *Las Delicias,* a large, neo-classic mansion on the outskirts of Alamos in the State of Sonora.

A graceful, soaring gate at the entrance to the atrium of a church in Querétaro
remains to show the love that craftsmen had for their work in Colonial times.
The art of casting iron has unfortunately become almost extinct in Mexico today.

A small embrasured window in the Bubelas' dining room in San Miguel de Allende has been imaginatively used to display a collection of turquoise blue Mexican glass.

Ascending to the romantic rooftops of Mr. Bejar's imagination is this noble cast-iron staircase. It probably came from a demolished XIX century townhouse.

Home of Feliciano Bejar

Home of Peter and Patricia Bubela

207

Home of Ignacio and Guadalupe Iturbe

Entering the dining room of the Iturbes' home in Mexico City, one is transported back into the early days of this century. With great sensibility, they have preserved intact not only the décor and furniture but also the art nouveau atmosphere of the room. The colorful leaded windows allow light to filter in through the turquoises, purples and greens of the rioting leaves and flowers of the design. To give it added light, the walls are painted a pale yellow, while the plaster decorations and the interiors of the niches at each end of the sideboard are left white.

Totally feminine, this beautifully worked wrought iron bed would not have looked out of place in any grand European country house of that period.

The owners of the Hacienda de "Ojo Caliente," in the State of Aguascalientes, are to be congratulated for keeping the Victorian decor and furnishings of their grand salon in such pristine condition. These rooms, which are still being used for their original purpose, preserve the traditions of the past in a warm and vital manner.

Hacienda de Ojo Caliente

Ex-Hacienda Museo de San Gabriel de Barrera

209

Vibrant and exciting color is the essence of the Tamayos' *sala*. Any attempt to describe the daring combinations and masterful results achieved in this room will be a pale effort. The floor of the simple, well-proportioned *sala* is tiled with unglazed terra-cotta *losetas* in a Spanish pattern. This rich, dark brown surface is covered by two thick wool rugs of a strong purple bougainvillea color. The cushions of the sofas are a dazzling chrysanthemum yellow. The roughly

Home of Rufino and Olga Tamayo

stuccoed white walls and the pale pink ceiling are brought into sharp contrast by the deep rose of the square niche, where polychromed wooden masks are displayed.

A large oval mirror, surmounted by two loving doves, adds to this rioting color scheme the burnished tones of gold.

Home of Christopher and Mary King

Arquitecto Manuel Parra has ingeniously used two large old tequila carafes to filter a soft greenish light into the King's monastic dining room.

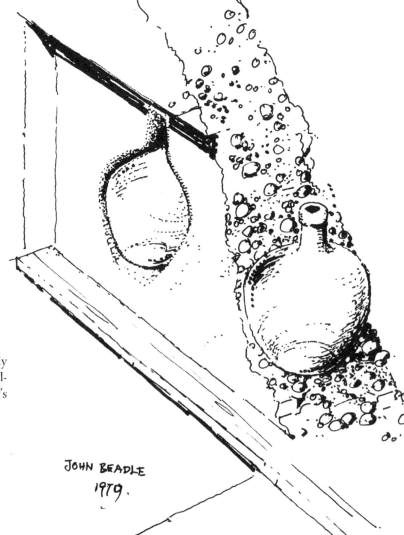

JOHN BEADLE
1979.

In the early XVI century, the Spanish established a primitive glass factory in Puebla. For some unknown reason, it was not a success, and the only reminder of these early efforts is a street in Puebla named *Calle del Vidrio*. However, in the XIX century, glass began to be made in Mexico. One of the oldest families dedicated to this craft is the Avalos clan, who nowadays own large factories for blown glass in Mexico City and in Guadalajara.

Home of Feliciano Bejar

The square glass bottles in Feliciano Bejar's kitchen are filled with all the delicious mysteries of Mexican cookery.

This endearing rounded bottle is known as an *Ojo de Boticario*. It served as an enlarging glass for old time druggists. These bottles are often found in small town drugstores, filled with vividly colored water.

Bazar Sabado

Similar in appearance to the famous Orrefors crystal, these attractive glass fish plates wait in the "Bazar Sabado" for someone to realize how lovely they would look on any table.

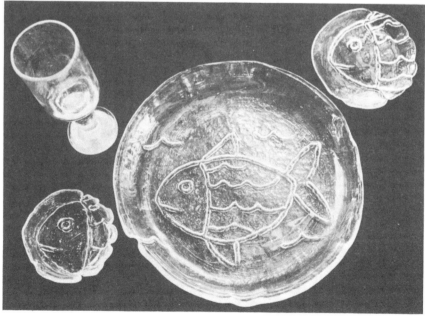

Jean Byron Fernández designed this delightful iron pot hanger which would add to the charm of any kitchen.

"Solo con Cita"

In the kitchen of Xavier Barbosa's ranch, large serving dishes and copper pots and jugs are handily displayed on these wood and wrought iron shelves.

Home of Xavier Barbosa

214

A collection of old Mexican pressed green glass looks striking against the terra-cotta color of this *nicho de concha*. All the different old measures for pulque, a rather sweet and potent drink made from a cactus, which natives imbibe with prodigious capacity, are shown here. With their amusing names, such as *Reina* (Queen), *Camión* (Truck), *Tornillo* (Screw), *Chivo* (Goat) and *Tripa* (Tripe), they invite Arquitecto von Waberer's guests to partake of this nectar of the Aztec gods.

Home of Jack and Muriel Wolgin

Home of Alejandro and Carmen von Waberer

A glowing brass towel rack of XIX century origin gives this small bathroom in a Cuernavaca home a discreet elegance.

215

Mexico is known for its beautiful metal and glass *faroles*. The designs that inspired these four hanging light fixtures are of Spanish Moorish and French origin.

Home of Alan and Jean Claire Salisbury

Under an antique glass *capelo* (dome) these two lovely XVIII century carved wood *Santos peregrinos* (Holy pilgrims) can be appreciated. This is just one of the many treasures in the Casa del Alfeñique in Puebla.

Interestingly designed, this pierced brass light fixture also serves to display an antique, blue-robed wood madonna.

Home of Robert and Violet Rice

A gaily painted tin and glass case holds an amusing collection of handmade little rag dolls.

Home of Rufino and Olga Tamayo

Home of Manuel and Teresa Barbachano Ponce

In an elegant dining room, an antique mirror which forms part of a carved
and gilded Colonial wood shelf, smokily reflects the candles on the mantelpiece.

Talented tinsmiths in San Miguel de Allende are responsible for these three intricately fashioned tin frames. The tall mirror with a contrasting bright and oxidized frame is in perfect harmony with the eclectic decor in James Ross Limantour's perfect living room.

Home of James Ross Limantour

Birds, fruits, owls and flowers are the sources of inspiration of the artisans who created these fascinating metal frames.

"Solo con Cita"

Sometimes using the most primitive tools, tinsmiths in Mexico are capable of producing marvels of design. Both the unique mesquite chair and the wooden chest benefit from their world of fantasy.

The brass and tin decorations on top of the chest are reminiscent of the paintings of well-known Guadalajara artist, Jorge Wilmott.

Home of Inez Havermale

Home of Jacques Baldassari

220

Platería Trejo

Velas Flamma

Maestro Sergio Trejo, armed with a pair of tin-cutting scissors, makes hundreds of these gay butterflies of all sizes. Once lacquered in bright colors, they are seen fluttering around in bathrooms, kitchens and nurseries, where they happily perch on curtains, lampshades and walls.

This black iron candleholder would look striking in any contemporary interior. Here, the fruit-like candles are yellow and orange, but they can be changed to accommodate the decor, the mood or the season.

The cook's humble bird and his distinguished companion, a ruffle-necked green and blue "rara avis," happily share this finely wrought wire cage.

Home of Peter and Patricia Bubela

221

Velas Flamma

Two silver-plated hurricane lamps that will make dining in the patio a romantic occasion. Yet another brilliant idea of the young designer who owns "Velas Flamma" in Mexico City and who has created a magical candle kingdom in his aromatic "Aladdin's Cave."

Home of Eleanor Lincoln

Home of Elton and Martha Hyder

A happy marriage of metals and glass have produced these three entrancing offspring. In the Hyders' guest room an antique brass bouquet of life-like fruit and flowers makes a stunning lamp base.

Peter Morris, an imaginative English painter and ceramist, designed and supervised the making of this repoussé tin light bracket.

222

The joyous spirit of the Fiesta of the Nativity is captured in the metallic color of the soaring *Cirio* (candle) of the village of Nauzontla in the State of Puebla. Created by native artisans out of multi-colored tinfoil cut in fanciful shapes, it is supported by a wax-encrusted wood framework and topped by four thin, decorated candles.

Its ephemeral life usually ends with the Fiesta. Fortunately, the museum in the former *Convento* de Santa Rosa and several private collectors have preserved some of these indigenous examples of popular art.

PAINT

THE SPANISH COLONIZERS were dazzled by the magnificence of the painted decorations that they found in palaces and temples when they arrived in Mexico in the early XVI century. Everywhere, marvels of composition met their eye and such a startling juxtaposition of strong colors that their conservative European souls must have been much alarmed. However, the monks who, with the aid of the natives, built marvelous *conventos* and churches, soon curbed these impetuous spirits and saw to it that the painted decorations of these buildings were more in tone with the somber religious concepts of the day.

In spite of these disciplines imposed on the natives, they introduced their own joyous love of color which, united with the Spanish sobriety, produced an exhilarating combination.

The same creative spark that urges the great muralists of our day to deliver their message through their work, impels the simple craftsman who earns his living by painting furniture and everyday objects to imbue them with his own inherent love of color.

High on a ladder, a self-taught artist happily paints his house in Tepoztlán with scenes of village life in the style of the Indians of Guerrero.

A touch of spring has been introduced into this elegant
living room by John Beadle's subtly-colored bouquets.

225

Home of Rufino and Olga Tamayo

Jaime Saldivar, of happy memory, dedicated this *retablo* to Rufino and Olga Tamayo with these words "Retablo dedicated with much love and affection to Rufino and Olga Tamayo as a homage to the best Mexican painter of all times and to Olga, his companion in love and in life."

The Tamayos' light and airy dining room is not only distinguished by the famous watermelons in the background, but also by the fascinating combination of pale lilac furniture and the thick purple bougainvillea-colored rug.

Home of Stewart and Alys Cort

Hotel La Mansión Galindo

Many are the rooms that John Beadle, a brilliant English painter and architectural designer, has painted in *trompe l'oeil*. This special art form consists of painting with precise naturalism to create the illusion that what is depicted is real.

This style of decoration often visually enlarges a room. The small rounded hall of the Corts' now looks impressively larger and has become the ornamental focal point of the house.

The large dining room of the luxurious "Hotel la Mansión Galindo" has also benefited from his talent. To this room he has given the light atmosphere of an XVIII century English country house. By introducing an overlaying green wooden trellis, he plays lightheartedly with the viewer's sense of reality.

One of his earlier efforts was painting the dining room of an elegant house in Mexico City. The result he achieved is so remarkable that guests are forever attempting to open the false door.

Home of the Marquis and Marquise de la Rozière

Home of Manuel and Teresa Barbachano Ponce

A garden of delights is depicted in this tall XVIII century painted screen that embellishes the Barbachanos' hall. Of great historic as well as esthetic interest, it illustrates with great precision the costumes and attitudes of people living in those times in Mexico.

231

Home of Manuel and Teresa Barbachano Ponce

Cecil O'Gorman, the author's grandfather and the father of famous muralist Juan O'Gorman, painted the small mural over a wooden garden gate and the doors leading into the library of the house he lived in (and which now belongs to Mr. and Mrs. Barbachano Ponce).

Home of Manuel and Teresa Barbachano Ponce

232

Home of Eddie Sleeswijk

Once made to be used as hope chests, these handsomely painted, fragrant wood boxes from the village of Olinalá in the State of Jalisco are now used to store records, extra blankets, old newspapers, bottled spirits, toys and any odds and ends.

Home of Rufino and Olga Tamayo

233

The romantic story of St. Christopher, patron saint of travelers, who carried the child Jesus across the swollen river, has been a perennial subject for artists through the ages. Here, on the wall of Mrs. Drewry's *zaguán*, he looms with benign authority.

Home of Marguerite Drewry

A blue and gold butterfly under a tender nosegay are part of the border of an original XVII century fresco in the former *Convento* of Santa Rosa in Puebla.

Placed under an antique linen church hanging, this simple low chest has been beautifully painted by Peter Morris. The two circular landscapes on the doors are surrounded by a gay leaf and flower border against a rich yellow background.

Home of Eleanor Lincoln

A great achievement in decoration is English artist Peter Morris's beautiful dining room in Mrs. Lincoln's house in Mexico City (*opposite page*). With taste and sensibility he designed the furnishings and repoussé tin light fixtures on the walls. He also painted the furniture and the frieze. Every piece of ceramic ware displayed in the niches and on the small side table was designed and decorated by him.

237

Home of Xavier Barbosa

Young misses during the last century were taught to ply their needles with great diligence and often produced small masterpieces. This softly colored and beautifully worked basket of flowers now adorns one of the guest rooms of the Rancho San Joaquín.

Home of Milton and Sabina Leof

An amusing anonymous Mexican Colonial painting of a child with a very sour expression hangs in the Leofs' lovely dining room in Cuernavaca. Against the hard blue-grey background, the delicate flesh tones and the light colors of the costume and of the flowers gleam softly.

Home of Alfonso and Feodora Rosenzweig Diaz

The unknown artist who painted this engaging scene of daily life in Mexico in the early 1800's shows a keen eye and a precise attention to detail. A señorita attended by her servants is enjoying the sweeping vista of Mexico City from her garden on the roof. In the foreground, a peasant woman is trying to interest them all in purchasing a cooling drink of whatever potion she is carrying on her back.

Home of Alejandro and Carmen von Waberer

By interspacing a letter between every beam, the artist completed the quotation from an early Spanish sonnet, *"Amor con amor se paga"* (Love can only be paid with love). Between every complete word he inserted a painted winged cherub's head.

Several of the wooden doors of the Casa del Alfeñique in Puebla are painted in this attractive way. After receiving two coats of matte "venetian red" paint, the design of the urns and the borders is superimposed in black and gold.

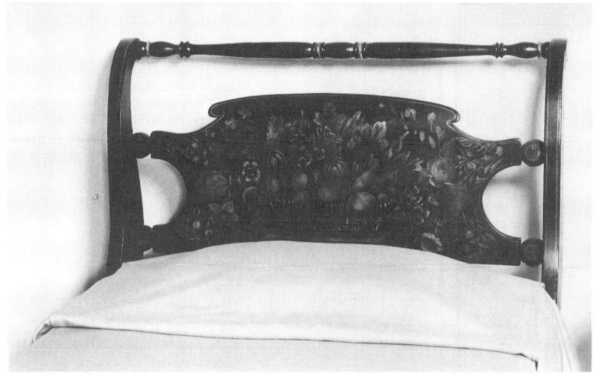

Three representative examples of a uniquely Mexican style of painted furniture known as *pera y manzana* (pear and apple), which was in vogue at the end of the XVIII century. The furniture was given an undercoating of either black or very dark olive green and the decorations of fruit or flowers were superimposed in other shades of green and in black. Gold leaf was used to shade and give depth to the design. Furniture painted in this way has now become treasured by collectors all over the country and an original piece in good condition is very difficult to find.

241

A simple screen shows one of the ways in which the ever-present tin *santos* can be displayed to great advantage. The oyster white antiqued finish of the wood makes an understated background for the many colors in the paintings.

A wealth of beautiful objects and fine paintings live together in perfect harmony in the *sala* of the Souzas' home in Mexico City. Antonio Souza, an art collector of vision and impeccable taste, has personally selected the furniture, paintings and objects in the room. The painted headboard depicts a gay al fresco meal, where the colorful figures and tall trees stand out clearly against the "venetian red" background.

Home of David and Anne Wilson   *Home of Antonio and Lala Souza*

Surrounding the tall side doors of the church in the mining village of Cata, near Guanajuato, is this large collection of painted *ex-votos*, a loving and personal way of thanking the black Christ to whom this church is dedicated. Each endearing little picture attests to some miraculous cure or divine intervention that saved a loved one from a horrible fate.

Cuernavaca Home
of Robert Brady

JOHN BEADLE '79 .

The high, massive tower that gives the house its name, *Casa de la Torre,*
was once part of the Bishop of Cuernavaca's palace in the XVI century cathedral
compound. Time has mellowed and enhanced its light apricot color and the
large *huamuchil* tree partly screens it with its delicate branches.

245

The "cantina" is in the base of the tower, which is the oldest part of the house. From this convivial spot, where the owner displays part of his collection of popular art, one can see the garden through an arch peopled with Guerrero pottery figures.

Below: The generous array of multicolored cushions on the long masonry benches have been collected by Mr. Brady on his travels throughout Africa and South America.

Beautifully placed in the semi-tropical Cuernavaca vegetation, the XVIII century wood statue of St. Peter can be appreciated from both the dining area on the terrace and the *Galería*.

247

These two primitive stone angels greet one's entrance into the lower hall with their welcoming and jubilant gestures.

Extraordinary advantage has been taken of the thickness of the Colònial wall in the dining room. Part of the stairway leading up to the *sala* is recessed into it. The wall behind the arch makes an ideal place to show ceramic plates, such as the large one in the center depicting a kangaroo and dating from the discovery of Australia. Part of Mr. Brady's large collection of pictures of San Pascual Bailón, the patron saint of cooks, two antique paintings set the wall aglow with their burnished tones.

Opposite: Painted in avocado green with a white pediment banded with a venetian red line, one of the arches in the *Galería* suitably frames Mr. Brady's personal artistic contribution. This wool and silk tapestry, entitled "Homage to Charles Prendergast," is one of his many creations and was woven in his own workshop. On the XVIII century wood chest below stand some of his choice ceramics and African sculptures.

Undoubtedly, the most fascinating place in the house is the *Galería*, an open-fronted, long, covered outdoor *sala*, where Mr. Brady does most of his entertaining. In this room he has placed some of the most interesting objects from his collections of furniture, archeological objects and primitive masks. The sloping beamed ceiling is supported by an extraordinarily long antique beam (*gualdra*) that runs the length of the entire room, and by four octagonal white stuccoed columns. Except for the *gualdra*, all the beams are painted venetian red and decorated on the underside with a dark green and white motif.

A fine red, orange, black and white North African rug lies in solitary splendor on the dark and richly polished floor. The giant square ceramic tiles were once part of the floor of a XVII century hacienda.

Cobalt blue, white and orange are the dominant colors of this kitchen. The alcove for the stove is tiled with antique *talavera* tiles which the owner discovered in Puebla. The two tile pictures of San Pascual Bailón also come from that city of legendary pottery and magical *azulejos*. A garland of garlic hangs above to frighten away bad spirits, which surely would hesitate to hover in so cozy a sanctum.

252

The owner's outstanding examples of Colonial art embellish the main hall on the second level of the high tower. A long, rectangular balcony and the tall open arch converted into a mirador are reminiscent of the enchanting Moorish lookouts in the gardens of Andalucía in Spain. Against the back wall, an early Colonial altar now provides a resplendent showcase for smaller objects. The standing figure of Christ in wood is of the XVII century.

CUERNAVACA HOME
OF ROBERT BRADY

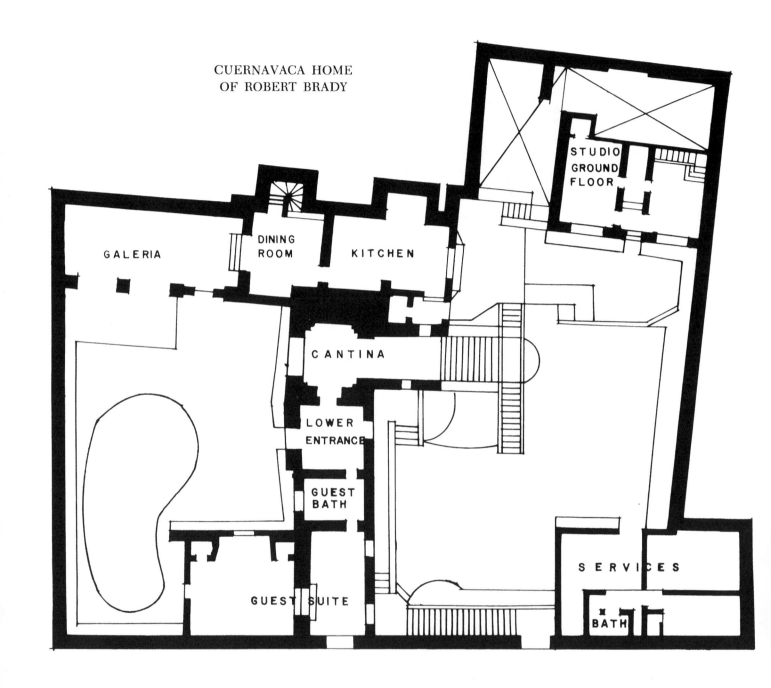

GALERIA

DINING
ROOM

KITCHEN

STUDIO
GROUND
FLOOR

CANTINA

LOWER
ENTRANCE

GUEST
BATH

SERVICES

GUEST SUITE

BATH

FLOOR PLANS

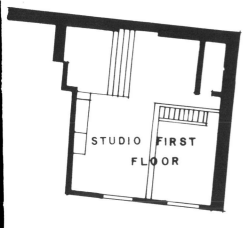

STUDIO FIRST
FLOOR

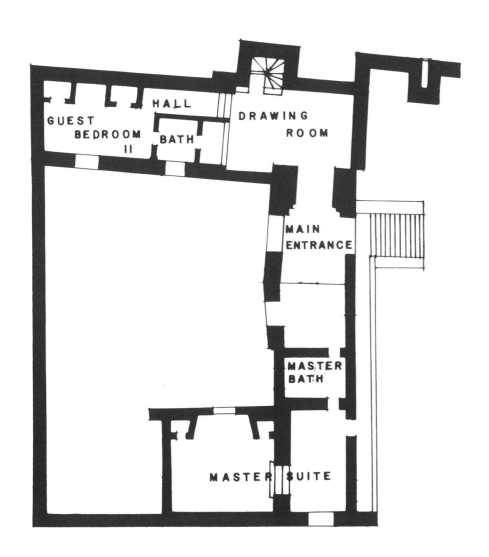

GUEST
BEDROOM
II

HALL

BATH

DRAWING
ROOM

MAIN
ENTRANCE

MASTER
BATH

MASTER SUITE

The clinging *moneda* (ficus) vine becomes a leafy green dress for the garden facade of the house.

Opposite: In a more contemporary style, the *sala* is also a most attractive room. By a brilliant use of color, Mr. Brady has made it light and welcoming. The ming yellow walls and curry-colored beams form an unassuming background for his fine collection of paintings which include a Tamayo still life painted in 1937 and works by Klee, Maurice Prendergast and Robert Henri. The chair, the back of which is indubitably a female figure, is a triumph of grotesquerie. It served originally as an orator's throne in the Sepik river area of New Guinea.

257

Home of Rufino and Olga Tamayo

Set into a simple mirrored frame, this joyous child, made by a native artist out of scraps of lace, colored paper and tinfoil, holds aloft the flag. One can almost hear her cry out, "*Viva México!.*"